SO-ABZ-982

DATE DUE

1264

group performance

davis

1264

Group Performance

Group Performance

JAMES H. DAVIS
University of Illinois

ADDISON-WESLEY PUBLISHING COMPANY
Reading, Massachusetts
Menlo Park, California · London · Don Mills, Ontario

TOPICS IN SOCIAL PSYCHOLOGY
Charles A. Kiesler, Yale University, Series Editor

Copyright © 1969 by Addison-Wesley Publishing Company, Inc. Philippines copyright 1969 by Addison-Wesley Publishing Company, Inc.

All rights reserved. No part of this publication may be reproduced, stored in a retrieval system, or transmitted, in any form or by any means, electronic, mechanical, photocopying, recording, or otherwise, without the prior written permission of the publisher. Printed in the United States of America. Published simultaneously in Canada. Library of Congress Catalog Card No. 74-91143.

HM
131
D36

For Stephen, Kristin, and Leah

Foreword

It is becoming increasingly difficult for anyone to be a generalist in social psychology. Not only is the number of articles published zooming, but new researchable areas of interest are multiplying as well. A researcher finds more fascinating topics these days than he used to, but he also finds himself behind in his reading of all but one or two of them. As a result, the quality of the broad introductory book in social psychology has suffered. No one can any longer be an expert in all of social psychology.

As an alternative, we offer the present series, *Topics in Social Psychology,* directed toward the student with no prior background in social psychology. Taken as a whole, the series adequately covers the field of social psychology, but it has the advantage that each short book was written by an expert in the area. The instructor can select some subset of the books to make up his course, the particular subset depending on his biases and inclinations. In addition, the individual volumes can be useful in several ways: as supplementary reading in, perhaps, a sociology course; to introduce more advanced courses (for example, a graduate seminar in attitude change); or just for peeking at recent developments in social psychology.

In this volume, James H. Davis attacks the classic problem of behavior and performance in groups. He includes a very cogent analysis of the comparison of individuals and groups, an issue that has always seemed to interest undergraduates especially. Discussions of group performance are seldom done well at this level, but I think you will find Dr. Davis' book a refreshing exception.

Charles A. Kiesler

Contents

CHAPTER ONE

Introduction

The investigation of group behavior poses problems not generally encountered in the study of individuals. The problems arise from the fact that a group is composed of several subjective processes. Each person reacts to a social situation in a rather different way, and there is no single conscious experience to call the group's own. In attempting to understand group phenomena, the early student of social behavior drew heavily upon his own experience in groups and upon his observations about the collective actions of others near and around him. Whereas the early experimental psychologist could supplement his own observations of behavior by requesting verbal reports from a subject responding to a stimulus selected by the experimenter, the early social psychologist found it impractical, for obvious reasons, to request a group to report directly on what "it" was doing. More recently psychologists have turned to direct and systematic observation of groups, but even this poses some very difficult measurement problems. If we were to consider at length the problems associated with the direct observation of active groups, we would discover that accurate observation and the acquisition of an orderly empirical record of interpersonal activities constitute troublesome difficulties that are still imperfectly resolved, even in the study of simple laboratory groups.

Our statement that there is no single conscious experience to call the group's own is one that would not always have seemed so self-evident. There was a time when crowds and mobs seemed so different from the individual's daily behavior that some tangible interpersonal linking or "extra-individual" phenomenon seemed to be the obvious explanation. Thus arose the notion of a kind of collective consciousness or *group mind*. Le Bon (1895), a sociologist-philosopher struck by the difference between the emotional and irrational quality of a person's actions in a crowd and his behavior in ordinary surroundings, felt that a kind of hypnotic trance engendered by the crowd must be the explanation. He believed crowds might release deep and dark passions within the individual, and that mob leaders worked their influence through emotion rather than reason. Various other mechanisms for the operation of the group as a collective consciousness were proposed by other students of collective behavior. The idea of a group mind can indeed be traced from the early nineteenth century to a high level of controversy in the 1920's.

As Cartwright and Zander (1968) have remarked, the dispute over the group mind had mainly to do with the "reality" of groups. According to one view, the group possessed attributes distinctly different from those of the component individuals, and its features were of a higher order and unique; groups could think, act, and decide. The contending view was that persons behaved, not groups, and that "group" as a concept lacked a firm empirical referent. Cartwright and Zander go on to point out (1968, p. 57):

> To most contemporary theorists, arguments about "reality" seem fruitless. A term like group mind is currently in disrepute, not so much because of reservations about the reality of groups, but because of its deficiencies as a scientific concept. It has never been clearly defined; neither its conceptual properties nor its empirical referents have been satisfactorily established. A term like group size, however, though referring to a collection of people, is readily accepted, since it is not difficult to conceive of feasible operations for ascertaining the number of people to be considered members of any particular group.

We shall not concern ourselves further with the group mind debate, except to point out that there is neither psychological nor physiological evidence that such a collective consciousness is in fact a palpable entity.

Over the past few decades the scientific study of group behavior has emerged as an increasingly important route to understanding. There seem to be two major reasons for that emergence. First, the development of logical tools for analyzing the simultaneous effects of many variables has proceeded at an increasing rate during recent decades. Modern statistical methods have aided the separation of jointly acting variables and their orderly interpretation in complex social situations. The second development has been the discovery that much social behavior can be studied in a controlled environment—the laboratory. Consequently, it has been possible to study group behavior under highly simplified circumstances. This is not to say that the phenomena under consideration in the laboratory are simple or devoid of relevance to larger social contexts and issues. On the contrary, the interplay between systematic field observation and laboratory investigation of complex social behavior has increasingly enriched our understanding of basic social processes wherever they occur.

The term "small group," while having no precise definition, has come to mean a set of a dozen or fewer people. Clearly, this is a relative matter, and no special importance is attached to deciding whether a particular group should be called small or large. However, there are a number of reasons for studying relatively small groups, other than that they are convenient or simple analogs of more complex forms. Foremost among these is the compelling fact that so much social life actually takes place within small, rather than large, groups. Reflect upon your past experience with other people. With how many people can and do you typically interact at one time on an intimate basis? Clearly, groups of 100 persons do not permit social interaction to any significant degree at the level of the full group. To be sure, a speaker may address thousands of people at a time; speeches may be programmed for each group member in turn; but acting and responding spontaneously in a natural fashion is simply out of the question in large sets of people. Consider what happens if we hold constant the time available for interaction, but gradually allow the number of people involved to increase indefinitely. If each person were accorded an equal share of time in which to hold the floor, even informally, the proportion of time available per member would become vanishingly small.

It is thus not surprising that formal or well-established large groups typically possess quite involved rules of procedure or custom to handle such problems as debate and decision making. One of the chief techniques available to large deliberative bodies, such as the U.S. Congress, is to create small groups (committees). The major business associated with problems of legislative action usually takes place in these small groups. Typically, meetings of the whole body are for formal voting and rituals concerning matters that have already been essentially decided prior to the general meeting.

A second illustration of the formation of smaller collectivities from a large one has probably been observed by anyone who has arrived at a party early. It is not uncommon for new arrivals to take their place in a large circle until the informal scheduling of conversation becomes laborious, even uncomfortable, and finally impossible. At some point, perhaps as the result of a fortuitous event, one can expect the large group to break up. People turn to neighbors and the buzz of conversation rises as groups of two and three persons converse animatedly among themselves.

In summary, the small group has become an object of intensive study for at least three reasons. (a) Small groups are simpler objects of study than are large groups. (b) Small groups are more easily subjected to experimental control. (c) The gathering of a limited number of people is a fairly common event in our culture, and such groups are the locus of perhaps the bulk of social life.

Definition of a Group

It is commonly observed that "group behavior" is a function of three classes of variables: (a) person variables, such as abilities, personality traits, or motives; (b) environmental variables that reflect the effects of the immediate location and larger organization, community, or social context in which group action takes place; and (c) variables associated with the immediate task or goal that the group is pursuing. There are a number of ways to classify groups, emphasizing one or the other of these three collections of variables. For example, Jennings (1950) has suggested that groups composed of persons who have sought and maintained membership primarily because they are interested in the goals of the group should be called *socio-groups;* groups composed of persons who are in the group mainly because they are attracted to the other members *per se* should be labeled *psyche-groups.* Since we are not aiming at an exhaustive treatment of the psychology of life in groups, we will not attempt to prepare a comprehensive listing of group types.

Groups may also be defined in many different ways (see Cartwright and Zander, 1968), and any group classification scheme is dependent to some degree on the definition chosen. For our purposes, we will choose to regard a human group as a set of persons (by definition or observation) among whom there exists a definable or observable set of relations. Thus the word "group" may not refer to a stable entity so much as the *place* of action or confluence of individual behavioral systems. A group is a set of mutually interdependent behavioral systems that not only affect each other, but respond to exterior influences as well. The notion of a group may seem less mysterious if it is imagined to be composed, first, of a set of persons, and second, of a collection of interdependent persons.

Group Performance

In this book we are concerned with what has been called group performance, group decision making, group problem solving, group productivity, group goal attainment, and a number of other things. The basic idea is that among the many reasons why people can and do get together in groups one major attraction is the collective pursuit of a particular end. The incidence of such task-oriented groups in our culture seems to be quite high. Legislative committees, industrial work groups, juries, boards of directors, and research teams are but a few examples of important classes of groups in our culture that aim to achieve particular ends. To be sure, such groups contain persons who, either formally or informally, take on quite different subtasks in the service of the overall goal. Nevertheless, the main thrust of the group is toward achieving some fairly definite outcome though perhaps not every member could clearly articulate the particular end result being sought.

We shall also emphasize the *experimental* study of task-oriented groups. The laboratory investigation of small groups reached a peak in the late 1950's, but since that time has figured less prominently in the study of social behavior. It has become increasingly evident (a) that the laboratory group is still a complex and difficult thing with which to work, and (b) that the group in a "natural" setting still has much to teach us. Much important social behavior is at present difficult or impossible to reproduce in the laboratory.

One increasingly popular research strategy has been to "remove" many social phenomena from a group setting altogether. A number of subtle social processes that underlie interpersonal behavior are currently studied in the laboratory without an accompanying group at all—conformity, aggression, and conflict, to name only a few. For example, just a few years ago the serious study of how bystanders respond to a victim needing prompt aid (Darley and Latané, 1968), of obedience to a command to hurt another (Milgram, 1965), and many other topics would have seemed hopeless in the laboratory. Such studies are now possible because it is no longer necessary to work with "real" groups.

Group Product, Structure, and Process

The study of small group performance has frequently been broken into three segments: (a) the group *product,* the output or response following work on some task or goal; (b) group *structure,* the pattern of interpersonal relations; and (c) group *process,* the activities that take place along the structural paths. Obviously, any attempt to segregate essentially overlapping and continuous phenomena rests on uncertain ground. Group behavior is a subject about which one would like to consider everything at once.

One important question concerns the fundamental unit of study within each of the above categories. Is it the group, the individual, or something else? Krech, Crutchfield, and Ballachey (1962) have suggested the "interpersonal behavioral event" as the fundamental unit for social behavior. Many conflicting opinions exist as to whether the individual or the group is the critical locus. Our approach in this book will be to emphasize *both,* and to stress not only the fruitfulness of contrasting individual with group performance, but also the desirability of ascertaining how disparate individuals turn into a recognizable group. This approach underlies the organization of the book. Taking as our fundamental interest the performance of some task, we shall consider in Chapter Two the contrast between isolated performers and similar persons confronted with an audience or noninteracting companions engaged in the same task. Our concern is less with the superiority of one setting over another than with the illustration and description of those features of the social environment that affect individual performance *per se.*

In Chapter Three we shall consider groups of *interacting* persons working collectively at a task. Again, we shall first take up the comparison of groups with individuals, but we will then focus on the primary question of how individual task-oriented behaviors are weighted, combined, or whatever in order to produce a distinct *group* product. There are several plausible "social combination rules" that one may conceive as corresponding to the interaction processes responsible for the group output.

In Chapter Four we will describe a few of the variables that are evidently related to group performance. Chapter Five takes up a kind of variable, group structure, that has such an important place in understanding group behavior that an entire chapter must be devoted to some aspects of the role it plays in the performing group.

Dependent Variables: an Overview

Dependent variables, which provide the raw material for the *in situ* study of groups, can be divided into three classes: (a) the task response *per se;* (b) the ongoing social interaction and its patterning; and (c) person variables, including both the individual's response to group activity (satisfaction, frustration, etc.) and his feelings about his own participation in the group.

Task response. Whether we consider the response of the individual member or the collective output of the group, there are only a limited number of measurements possible. One datum is the latency or time lapse between presentation of the task or stimulus and the contingent answer or response.

A second kind of datum is the quality of the answer: the specific category of response. The system of response categorization is determined largely by the researcher and the particular problem being presented. A very common categorization system is simply a correct-incorrect dichotomy, where the criteria for sorting answers into these two classes are determined by logic (for example, in an arithmetic problem), by the environment (where it is clear that a certain thing is empirically true), or by an experimenter who controls the feedback following a response sequence. However, many group problems do not fall into such a neat system; hence, the investigator may be more interested in the way responses are distributed across a *set of categories* or along a *continuum.* Group decision problems are frequently of the latter sort. There is often no easy way to label answers correct or incorrect, and frequently the major task facing the group is agreement on *any* response at all.

A third way of treating group output for some tasks is to tabulate the number or quality of units produced per unit time. In other words, the previous variables are sometimes combined at this point, enabling task results to be analyzed in terms of such things as the rate of errors or "creativity" of solutions.

Social interaction. These three types of response measurement (latency, quality, and rate of response) can also be applied to groups in which the immediate stimulus for a member's behavior is another person or other persons, rather than some problem facing the group. However, the application of the notions of latency, quality, and rate of response to this kind of group has been less clearly analyzed, perhaps because such a problem is uniquely social-psychological and consequently fewer techniques are available from earlier work with individual subjects. Social interaction, by definition, does not actually exist prior to grouping, except as tendencies or propensities in the individual person.

Leaving aside for the moment the assessment of such individual propensities or traits, it is possible to distinguish two basic means for obtaining data concerning interpersonal behavior: (a) the observation of interpersonal behavior by trained observers and (b) the self-report of the individual member concerning his own reaction to others and his perceptions of the reactions of fellow group members to each other. Actually, a third source of interpersonal data exists, but it has been exploited to a rather small degree. This third source consists of (c) the "traces" left behind by the interaction itself (see Webb, Campbell, Schwartz, and Sechrest, 1966). The seating preferences of group members, the physical distance between persons in a face-to-face group, and the route chosen for sending messages in groups not in a face-to-face relation are all examples of "self-recording" traces that sometimes permit an investigator to reconstruct the type and pattern of interpersonal relations obtaining during group activities.

Person variables. Information concerning group members centers on two categories of data: (a) situation or group-dependent responses (for example, morale), and (b) relatively stable personal features (for example, general intelligence). In general, the assessment of individual persons involved in group activity differs in no fundamental way from assessment in other areas of psychology that routinely employ interviews, expert ratings, or questionnaires. The problem for investigators of group performance is that of finding opportunities for obtaining such data. Testing subjects immediately prior to group work often has the potential difficulty of biasing the subject's performance during group interaction; postgroup measurement has an equal but opposite effect of potentially yielding test results unduly dependent on the immediately preceding group activity. As a rule, personality variables should be assessed independently of the laboratory study of the group members. Unfortunately, such data are often not available, and thus much of the research that focuses on groups does not also deal with detailed data pertinent to the individual group member.

CHAPTER TWO

Individual Performance in a Social Context

The basic study of small group performance has generally focused on tasks that are fairly complex and involve abstract cognitive processes to a significant degree. There have been a number of exceptions; in the early years of experimental social psychology, groups were often presented with tasks requiring fairly simple responses or routine motor performance. However, it is obvious that a task-oriented group chosen at random from real life is likely to be working at something which in fact requires a mixture of psychological processes for its resolution.

We have already indicated that this book is primarily concerned with group output and with the social processes that are responsible for it. Much group research, however, has been carried out with a reverse emphasis in which the central focus has been on interpersonal processes, the group goal being of secondary interest. In either case, one must be concerned not only with the manner whereby the social process combines individual contributions into a group response, but also with the way the individual's contribution is influenced by the social context. We shall consider this latter issue in the next section.

THE SOCIAL CONTEXT

It is hardly surprising that psychologists, with their emphasis on individual behavior, should at a very early stage in the experimental study of social behavior have asked how *individual* task performance compares with *collective* performance. This is a fairly broad question, for many personal and interpersonal variables are cloaked by the term "collective." Nevertheless, subsequent attempts to answer some form of the individual-versus-group question have led to both empirical and theoretical advances. These attempts may be categorized into one or more of three variations on the basic question: (a) How does the *mere presence* of others, such as a passive audience of one sort or another, affect the task performance of a single subject? (b) How does the presence of *coactors,* such as other persons ⊁ engaged simultaneously in the same task but working independently, affect the performance of a single subject? (c) How does *interaction* with others, in various forms, affect the performance of the single subject? We may assume that the complexity of the question increases with each category, for the effects on performances observed in an earlier category would presumably be included in a later one. The first two categories will be considered together in this chapter, and the third will be taken up later in connection with the production of *collective* solutions to a task.

The labeling of social variables as "social context effects" or "grouping phenomena" is a rather gross kind of characterization; but it is one that has been used by earlier researchers, and it points vaguely to important considerations that the student of group behavior cannot overlook. Another justification for concerning ourselves with mere audience or coaction effects has to do with the widespread notion that task and social environment represent rather distinct sets of behavioral determinants. Collins and Guetzkow (1964) have suggested that task-environmental stimuli be considered one class of performance determinants, and that the interpersonal environment of each person be considered another. Within each category there are both task-environmental obstacles and rewards and social-interpersonal obstacles and rewards.

AUDIENCE EFFECTS

Although the very earliest studies used coacting subjects, the audience effect is conceptually simpler, and hence we shall consider it first. Despite the fact that some research has failed to show that audiences produce a consistent improvement or decrement on some task (e.g., Gates, 1924), the great bulk of the evidence suggests that the knowledge that others are present or will soon be present to observe one's work does have a strong effect on performance. For example, Travis (1925) required subjects to hold a flexible pointer in contact with a target located on a revolving disc (the pursuit rotor apparatus). Practice, carried out alone except for the presence of the experimenter, continued for several days until the task was well learned. Then, after a warmup period, each subject was required to perform in front of a passive audience that varied in size from four to eight persons. Although most subjects were judged to demonstrate distress to some degree or other, more than 80 percent of the subjects performed better in front of the audience than alone. As Zajonc (1966) points out in his discussion of the Travis study, the average difference in performance scores between all alone trials and all audience trials, and between the best alone trials and the best audience trials, favored the audience trials, but the differences were not great. A number of similar findings have been reported. For example, Ichheiser (1930) discovered that audiences enhanced accuracy and speed on several performance tests.

When queried informally, most experienced athletes indicate that performing before a "real" audience, in a game or at a meet, facilitates feats of strength, endurance, and physical output. Another informal datum comes from a common class demonstration using a subject who has had some practice in the Minnesota Rate of Manipulation Task (a board containing rows of round pegs that are to be picked up one at a time, turned over, placed in the other hand, and replaced in the hole as quickly as possible). If allowances are made for some initial warmup, performance on this task increases substantially when the peg turner is required to perform in front of his own or a different class.

Many of the original experiments using audiences dealt with skill and motor performance of some sort. Currently such an emphasis is most likely to be found in research having an applied focus, such as in industrial settings where facilitation of output or monitoring of test equipment has important consequences (e.g., Latané and Arrowood, 1963).

In general, the notion that an audience facilitates performance appears to have been well supported in several areas of investigation. However, we have mainly considered very simple tasks, especially those involving routine motor performance. Motor skills are likely to be "overlearned," and hence require little conscious effort or abstract "processing" of information between task presentation and consummatory response.

The presence of an audience does not always result in facilitation; evidence of social inhibition also exists. For example, Wapner and Alper (1952) presented subjects with a particular passage and a pair of words. The subjects were then required to select the word that they believed to be more consistent with the passage. Subjects' decisions were timed in each of three experimental conditions: (a) deciding alone, except for an experimenter; (b) deciding before an audience of other students and a faculty member who could be seen on the other side of a window; and (c) deciding before an unseen audience, previously described to the subject, on the other side of a one-way window. On the average, decision times were shortest for subjects who were alone, and longest for subjects performing before an *unseen* audience. The observable-audience condition fell between these two. The subjects apparently began to adapt during the course of the experiment; on the average, differences between conditions were negligible by the end of the approximately one-hour session.

The Wapner and Alper experiment is interesting for a number of reasons. First, the *kind* of audience seems to play an important role in the degree of social facilitation or inhibition. Wapner and Alper thought the unseen audience represented more of a threat to "self-status" than did the audience which was visible to the performers. In addition, the average decision time of the subjects in this experiment was *inhibited* by a group of passive observers. Note that in this case the task was rather complex, requiring the respondent to make a decision after considering the nature of the initial phrase presented to him.

Audiences need not always be passive. They may react to a performer in a wide range of ways, as we see in athletic contests. The audience response may vary from actively critical through indifferent to supportive. Taking the negative extreme as an example, we find relevant evidence in a study by Laird (1923). In Laird's experiment, fraternity pledges performed several different tasks. We shall consider only two of the tasks, speed of tapping and steadiness in "standing." In accord with arrangements made by the experimenter, each pledge appeared before the assembled active members of the fraternity, who subjected him to vicious "razzing" and derogation. In comparison with a control series of measurements on each subject, in which the fraternity members were passive spectators, the razzing produced a substantial decline in performance. Though decline was almost uniformly the case for steadiness standing scores, several pledges actually improved their tapping rate in front of the actively unpleasant audience. While the generally inhibitory effect of a negative audience is hardly surprising, the kind of task the subject is required to perform again appears to be a crucial factor, at least for some persons.

Let us consider further the matter of task type. A strict learning task represents, on the face of it, quite a different set of requirements from many of those mentioned previously. Pessin (1933) had subjects learn lists of nonsense syllables alone and in front of a passive audience. For the comparison in which we are interested, it turned out that, on the average, learning a sequence of seven nonsense syllables was faster when the subject was alone than when in front of spectators. Moreover, the mean number of errors during acquisition was larger when a passive audience was present than when the subject was alone. We shall return to this experiment later, for it has been analyzed in such a way as to explain what appear to be many conflicting results.

It should be evident by now that an individual performing before an audience is sometimes likely to "do better" than when alone and sometimes likely to "do worse," but is rather unlikely to be indifferent to the presence of others. If this were all that could be said after so much work—and we have only sampled the voluminous literature in our discussion—the statement would perhaps be valuable, but not very exciting theoretically. Fortunately, we will see that the diversity of findings, and even the outright contradictions, can generally be explained by a simple but rather elegant theoretical principle.

First, however, we will consider the second variation on the basic individual-versus-group question: namely, *coaction*. It is clear that even the simple "mere audience" situation is highly complex, and actually cloaks a number of important task-social considerations relevant to human performance. The mere audience effects would have perhaps seemed even more conflicting and bewildering if we had chosen to emphasize individual differences in work attitudes and personality traits.

COACTION EFFECTS

Since the behavior of a single person is greatly affected by the knowledge, or even suspicion, that others are regarding his performance in some way, it is likely that as the "presence variable" is made more salient its role in determining performance will in turn increase. Indeed, Laird's study of "razzing" leads directly to such a conclusion. The importance of others may be increased in various conceivable ways, such as when they are perceived as competitors or allies, sources of information, sources of rewards and punishments, and sources of emotional support or personal regard. The simplest case will be considered in this section: that in which the purposeful *interaction* is at a minimum. The "others" now become performers of the same or related tasks, but they do not interact directly with the subject in the pursuit of that task. Such coactors, however, turn out to be far from insignificant or inert as sources of social stimulation.

Just as we found the mere-presence or passive-audience paradigm to be far more complex than appeared on the surface, so does the coaction paradigm turn out to be more complex than at first appears. The coaction paradigm has received substantial attention, and the amount of relevant experimental research exceeds that done with passive audiences. Part of the reason for this appears to be practical. Competition and "individualism" are recurrent themes in western culture, and this fact raises a number of questions. Does competition or cooperation yield a better product in terms of quality, or speed, or both? Do students learn better at school together or apart? The practical emphasis also explains the rather atheoretical approach that was taken initially, for the basic aim was simply to discover whether performance was "better" together or apart. For example, more than 35 years ago, Murphy and Murphy (1931) summarized the already considerable literature on the "individual in the group situation" and noted (p. 458) that

> ... the background of the exceedingly important problem of the difference between the execution of a task alone and the execution of the same task in the presence of others lies, as Allport has pointed out, in the work of German educators, notably Mayer (1903), Schmidt (1904), and Meumann (1914). In general, the investigations (which have been continued and confirmed) indicate that classroom work is more stimulating than home work, although the latter may be bettered by the use of special incentives.

Even earlier, Triplett (1898), a cycling enthusiast, observed informally that cyclists racing against time were inferior to those racing against some sort of pacer. The paced performers were, in turn, inferior to those racing against actual competitors. Triplett entertained a number of explanatory hypotheses, but favored the idea that the presence of others stimulated previously formed associations between sight and action such that riding responses were directly stimulated, thereby saving the subject the effort of being constantly "on guard." Triplett also found that other competitive sports yielded informal data similar to those he had collected from his observations of cyclists.

Triplett followed his field observations with a laboratory experiment in which 40 children (aged 8 to 17 years) wound fishing reels alone and in competition with others. Twenty subjects performed better in the "together" than in the "apart" condition; 10 subjects did worse, and 10 were virtually the same in the two conditions. Triplett considered that stimulation is helpful, but that overstimulation could be detrimental. Overstimulation was considered the reason why some of the children did worse when together. Variations in performance and cramped muscles were cited as supporting evidence for this interpretation.

Although the average improvement in speed was quite small for Triplett's subjects, subsequent research tended to confirm his findings. As Hare (1962, p. 346) has observed,

> . . . some children are stimulated positively by the presence of others while some are not (Shevaleva & Ergolska, 1926). In general, children seem to find the together situation more stimulating than do adults (Feofanov, 1928). Subjects with low intelligence are less stimulated (Abel, 1938) than the more intelligent. Under social influence, subjects were observed to be more active but less accurate at the beginning of a task such as printing or putting pegs in a board (Sengupta & Sinha, 1926; Anderson, 1929; Leuba, 1933; Dashiell, 1930, 1935). A similar effect was observed when a second subject was added after the first subject was satiated with the task (Burton, 1941). Subjects were less likely to become bored if others were working at the same task (Taylor, Thompson, & Spassoff, 1937).

Triplett's subjects were coacting, but in a sense they might also be said to have been minimally interacting; for the introduction of competition set up a kind of interpersonal contingency in that one's own performance was evaluated in connection with what others did. Subsequent research tended to control the competition factor to some degree, as well as a number of other important variables.

One of the earliest and most important names associated with the area of "together" and "apart" studies was that of F. H. Allport (1924). Allport explored the area that came to be known somewhat loosely as "social facilitation," and drew attention to the distinction between coacting and interacting groups. Through careful experimentation, he discovered that coaction can be inhibiting as well as facilitating, and that substantial individual differences exist in susceptibility to such effects. Moreover, Allport tended to work with adults, whereas earlier researchers were prone to use children as subjects. He also tended to place a somewhat greater emphasis on abstract thought processes, whereas motor skills and simple responses had predominated in the tasks chosen for much previous experimental research.

Allport attempted to minimize implied competition by avoiding score comparisons or any reference to rivalry in instructions or experimental procedure. Thus his studies fit our initial interest in simple coaction very well. Alternating between together and apart conditions, subjects were tested on "free chain associations" in which they were to write as many words as possible after seeing the stimulus word that appeared at the top of a page. Almost all subjects gave more associations when seated together about a table than when alone in separate rooms. The social increment was much stronger in the earlier portion of the group work than in the later portions—an effect frequently observed with passive audiences. In addition, coacting subjects gave fewer personal associations than when alone, and were apparently more likely to incorporate immediate environmental events into their association chain. In a separate but otherwise similar experiment, Allport attempted to decrease the amount of writing required of respondents; he found that the general social facilitation effects decreased and that variability of performance increased when subjects were together.

Although word associations represent somewhat abstract psychological processes, these processes are still presumably much simpler than those that would be required by reasoning tasks; moreover, the main dependent variable in Allport's experiments was speed of response. Consequently, it is of special interest to note that Allport considered the quality of thought in an experiment involving a more complex task: subjects in "alone" and "together" conditions were required to write, in a limited time, some counterarguments to selected passages from Marcus Aurelius and Epictetus. He found that while coactors generally wrote *more* counterarguments to a stimulus passage than did "alone" subjects, the judged quality of the proposals was typically superior for subjects working alone. It is interesting to note that Allport's research has often been used as evidence for the superiority of group work, despite the fact that coaction was facilitating for vowel cancelation, chain association, and simple multiplication, but *not* facilitating for the abstract counterarguments task just described.

Allport's experiments, along with others, led to the general conclusion that "grouping" tends to facilitate average speed of performance, to inhibit the quality of work, and to provoke substantial variability in both quality and speed. Moreover, Allport thought that coworkers tended to facilitate *overt* responses, such as writing, and to inhibit *implicit* responses, such as would be most evident in abstract thought. In any event, it is clear that subjects are affected by social stimuli, as well as other environmental factors, in their performance of particular tasks, and that this effect appears to move from benign to harmful as the "complexity" of the task increases. Before considering the key role of the task stimulus further, we might take note of Kelley and Thibaut's summary (1954, p. 750) dealing with the comparison of a subject alone with a subject working *either* in a coacting situation or before a passive audience. Working in a social context results in:

(a) Greater quantity of work where physical output is involved, suggesting increased motivation to perform the task. (b) Lesser quantity or quality of work where intellectual processes or concentration are involved, suggesting that social stimuli are able to compete successfully with the task stimuli. (c) Inhibitions of responses and qualitative changes in the work, which suggest that the person somehow "takes account" of the others as he goes about his work, e.g., he has fewer idiosyncratic thoughts, exercises moderation in judgement, and gives more "popular" or common associations. (d) Greater variations through time in his output, indicating the presence of periodic distractions and/or the effects of working under greater tension. (e) There is some evidence that these effects wear off as the person adapts to the social situation.

Just as we found that changes in the audiences and/or changes in the subject's perception of them altered his performance, so do we find that changes in one's *coactors* have a strong influence on individual performance. One obvious coactor behavior that would be of interest is competition. In fact, it is tempting to think that audience *and* coaction effects might be traceable to implicit competition and hence heightened motivation. However, as we have seen, several reversals of the social facilitation effect due to grouping would still need to be explained.

Dashiell (1930) instructed subjects to work *both* as accurately and as rapidly as possible. He then studied subjects (a) alone in front of passive, attentive spectators, (b) together with simple coactors, and (c) together with competing coactors. Although performance on multiplication problems, a mixed relations test, and free serial work associations varied within and across each condition, Dashiell concluded that the competitive attitude was the most important influence, far outweighing in importance what he called the "ideomotor" factor as a cause of social facilitation. (The ideomotor factor was considered to be a kind of "autosuggestion" that arose in connection with emotional factors elicited by a social situation.)

One is tempted to seek the resolution of the sometimes consistent, but often conflicting, findings on social facilitation and inhibition in personal idiosyncrasies and subtle environmental influences, unintentionally varied from investigator to investigator. Indeed it is easy to document the fact that a positive attitude toward the task or audience-coactors facilitates performance and a negative attitude inhibits. The perceived positive regard of audience-coactors facilitates performance, especially speed, and negative regard inhibits.

This is where the matter of task performance in a social context stood until quite recent theoretical and experimental innovations brought substantial order to our observations derived from audience and coacting situations. From the late 1930's until the late 1960's, the bulk of individual-group research was concerned less with task performance than with the social context—especially the social relations that developed or were manipulated. This trend away from task performance *per se* was recognized in 1954 by Kelley and Thibaut, who also accurately forecast that it would continue.

AUDIENCE-COACTION EFFECTS
AND AROUSAL IN THE PRESENCE OF OTHERS

Although Allport (1924) had concluded that overt responses are facilitated and implicit responses inhibited by others, it remained for Zajonc (1965, 1968) to reopen the basic question and advance an important explanatory notion. Zajonc observed a subtle consistency in the apparently conflicting results of the "together-apart" paradigm which we have been considering: namely, that the performance which was *facilitated* involved tasks requiring *well-learned behavior;* social *inhibition* occurred where the *acquisition of new information* was required by the task. Why should this be so? Before discussing this question, let us consider examples for both the audience and coaction experimental paradigms to see how the acquisition-recall generalization fits the available evidence.

At this point we are concerned only with the presence of others, not with the subject's attitude or his use of others as sources of information, cues to appropriate behavior, or models for learning. We mentioned earlier the Pessin (1933) experiment in which subjects who learned nonsense syllables in front of a passive audience were inferior to subjects who learned the same list alone. Our discussion was incomplete, for subjects in that experiment were tested again later. In the later testing, the task was to relearn the original list alone or in front of a passive audience. The results were quite clear. Substantially fewer trials were required to relearn in the audience condition than in the alone condition. In general, the results from experiments using the alone and passive-audience conditions, as exemplified by this study, are quite clearly in accord with Zajonc's notion: passive audiences facilitate well-learned responses. If the well-learned response is also the correct one, we speak of socially facilitated performance; if the emitted response is "incorrect," we speak of socially inhibited performance.

We might follow Zajonc at this point and emphasize the importance of a common distinction in psychological terminology, that between *learning* and *performance.* Learning is the acquisition of new responses, and performance is the emission of old (that is, well-learned) ones. Earlier it seemed that motor skills or overt acts were likely to be socially facilitated, while implicit responding would be inhibited. This, too, is consistent with Zajonc's formulation, for physical-motor skill tasks are likely to require little more than already learned responses, while problems, by definition, imply that the subject has no immediately forthcoming goal-oriented response (Johnson, 1955). The problem solver must acquire new information or learn a new arrangement of old information already in storage. (In this book, the term performance is used to refer to all behavior that is primarily stimulated by the task, as opposed to socially instigated behavior.)

If we consider the coaction paradigm, the story is much the same, except that most coaction research has not ruled out the possibility of one's coactors serving as information sources themselves, thereby compensating for and even overriding the coaction effects. Most learning tasks that are facilitated by the presence of coactors, thereby offering conflicting evidence for the proposition we are entertaining (see Gurnee, 1939, 1968), seem to admit of some learning-by-observation. Of course, imitation learning and other vicarious phenomena are important grouping effects in their own right, and we will discuss them later.

In any event, Zajonc (1965) has interpreted the Allport coaction experiments (which found chain word association, vowel cancellation, reversible perspective rates, and multiplication to be facilitated, but problem solving and judgment to be unimproved, by coactors) to be consistent with his explanation (pp. 269-274):

> Word association, multiplication, the cancellation of vowels, and the reversal of the perceived orientation of an ambiguous figure all involve responses which are well established. They are responses which are either very well learned or under a strong influence of the stimulus, as in the word-association task or the reversible-perspective test. The problem-solving test consists of disproving arguments of ancient philosophers. In contrast to the other tests, it does not involve well-learned responses. On the contrary, the probability of wrong (that is, logically incorrect) responses on tasks of this sort is rather high; in other words, wrong responses are dominant. . . . Therefore, the generalization proposed . . . can again be applied: if the presence of others raises the probability of dominant responses, and if strong (and many) incorrect response tendencies prevail, then the presence of others can only be detrimental to performance.[*]

What is it about the mere presence of others that promotes the emission of responses dominant in the individual's behavioral repertoire? Zajonc (1965, 1968) suggests that the presence of others is a source of general arousal or activation. It has frequently been proposed that such drive concepts indeed have the property of increasing the probability of elicitation of the well-learned (dominant) response from among those

---

[*]Copyright 1965 by the American Association for the Advancement of Science.

available—in other words, of fostering performance. By definition, performance is "poor" early in learning, for incorrect responses are dominant; after selective reinforcement over a number of trials, the response chosen for reinforcement is learned or dominant. Subsequent performance is thus "good" in that the responses selected by the experimenter's plan or logic are the most probable under sufficient motivation.

Is the presence of coactors or an audience arousing to the performers? Zajonc is careful to point out that the evidence is mainly indirect, citing research with animals ranging across a wide variety of species: ants (Chen, 1937), chickens (Bayer, 1929), rats (Harlow, 1932), to name only a few. In nonhuman studies the evidence is frequently physiological. For example, adrenocortical activity is known to increase during arousal, and elevated hydrocortisone levels have been observed in groups of animals under a variety of conditions, especially in very densely populated though otherwise adequate environments. We might observe informally that a high level of arousal is commonly reported by actors and public speakers, even when they are appearing before a supposedly friendly audience. In addition, such reports usually include the feeling that there is a decline, all other things being equal, in the level of this arousal with time spent in the performance. We have, of course, observed in several experiments that the audience and coaction effects seem to run a time course in that they level off even during so short a time as that consumed by the typical experiment—perhaps an hour or two, on the average.

However, some slight but rather direct evidence for arousal induced by the presence of others does exist. Shapiro and Leiderman (1964) have described their use of heart rate and galvanic skin response as indicators of emotional state within socially active individuals. The galvanic skin response (change in the electrical conductivity of the skin) has long been regarded as a measure of central nervous system arousal or general activation. While this measure provides no evidence on the subjective quality of the subject's emotional state, it does reflect the intensity of the arousal. Heart rate, on the other hand, is more closely associated with internal or maintenance activities than with changes in the external environment. Shapiro and Leiderman (1967) used both indices as direct measures of physiological changes associated with the manipulation of social and task reinforcement variables.

Working partly from the idea that audiences and coacting subjects are arousing, Shapiro and Leiderman required subjects to guess which one of several colors would be presented on each of several trials by an experimenter. Subjects were either "correct" or "incorrect" on a high proportion of the trials. Actual success and failure were irrelevant, for the experimenter arranged the feedback to be experimentally convenient. In addition, subjects were seated in three-person groups about a table, and although they could hear each other's guesses, they were not permitted to

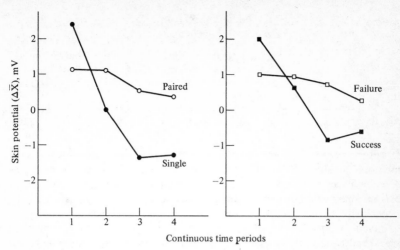

Fig. 2.1 The relationship between arousal, as measured by GSR, and (a) the presence of others and (b) amount of success. (From Shapiro and Leiderman, 1967. Copyright 1967 by the American Psychological Association, and reproduced by permission.)

discuss their decisions about the color of the next card. They were instructed that as soon as one person saw the word "start" he was to announce his color choice, and then all three were simultaneously to press their buttons corresponding to the colors they had personally selected. By a suitable manipulation of the interpersonal contingencies, two different group settings were contrived in which two subjects were successful and the third a failure, or two were a failure and the third a success. Thus there were two levels of task performance (success and failure) and two levels of interpersonal-task contingency (paired and single).

Shapiro and Leiderman found that mean galvanic skin response declined over the 45-minute experimental period, as had been observed or inferred from previous studies dealing with arousal effects. More important, the decline in arousal was faster for single subjects than for paired subjects; that is to say, the mean galvanic skin response dropped off less rapidly for pairs than for singles. The decline was also faster for the success subjects than for the failure subjects. Thus pairing and success moderated the "usual" adaptation in arousal. These results are presented graphically in Fig. 2.1.

To be sure, the design used by Shapiro and Leiderman does not address itself to the "together-alone" paradigm directly, for all subjects were together in the obvious sense that they were tested within sight and hearing of each other. However, the findings at least show an important contingency between arousal and social context.

Concluding Remarks
on Passive Audiences and Coaction

We have discussed at some length the findings concerning situations which afford distinctly minimal social confrontation. We have done so for three reasons:

1.   Despite their apparent simplicity, audience and coaction settings turn out to exert powerful and rather complicated effects on the individual person.

2.   For psychology, these social circumstances represent both historically and conceptually a point of "crossing over" from an emphasis on individual behavior to an emphasis on collective behavior. Moreover, there is perhaps a clearer continuity between "general" and social psychology than has been recognized in the past, and the principles of one may sometimes be extended directly to the other. In general, the comparison of individuals with groups serves to illustrate the futility of the old argument that phenomena at one level (social) of abstraction *should* not be explained by concepts at the next lower (individual) level. The more important question is: *Can* they be so extended? And if so, are they really very helpful in furthering the important goals of understanding and predicting social behavior?

3.   Finally, our discussion has served to illustrate in a forceful way the utility of theory itself. It is difficult to overestimate the importance of Zajonc's notion of socially originating arousal for organizing past results, guiding future research, and reviving interest in an obviously important but recently neglected area.

When the task assigned to isolated subjects and to subjects performing before audiences requires *both* routine responses and learning, there appear to be some rather puzzling and complex effects not entirely predictable from arousal theory (Davis, Carey, Foxman, and Tarr, 1968). However, the evidence is currently rather scanty for this undoubtedly very common sort of task, and we will not discuss such effects further here. In the future, it will be necessary to develop some means for effectively controlling the ratio of routine performance to learning demands associated with the task.

THE INDIVIDUAL'S USE OF OTHERS' BEHAVIOR

Man is not alone in his dependence on collective action and social organization as a means of furthering his adaptation to the environment. A wide range of species exhibit a significant degree of social life, up to and including man himself. With few exceptions, primates are generally characterizable as social creatures, and much of their social behavior depends on *experience* with others rather than instinct alone. Indeed it is hard to escape the conclusion that grouping in its various forms does something important for the adaptive economy of many organisms. We have just explored a motivational consequence (arousal) of grouping that may even be considered to foster adaptation on some occasions. Although we do not wish to pursue "social Darwinism" formally at this point, we shall now consider briefly two additional functions that the mere presence of others appears to serve for the individual:

a)   The behavior of other persons serves as a source of cues or information about what behavior is *desirable* or *permissible,* and sometimes even provides a *model* for how one might actually perform an act.

b)   The mere presence of others represents a source of *comfort* or *support* in the face of anxiety provoked perhaps by some threat to the individual.

The first function is usually discussed under the rubric of social learning or imitation, and the second traditionally falls within the general area of social motivation and emotion. In neither case will we consider "others" as interacting directly with the single individual, such as by providing intentional reinforcement or comforting comments in conversation.

Other Persons as Models or Sources of Information

Observational learning and imitation. In a sense, we have switched the roles of the single performer and his multiperson audience. We are now inquiring as to how the *passive observation* of others performing some act affects an audience of one; we are still not concerned with interaction, at least in the direct sense. Thus our concern is primarily with *vicarious* events taking place within the observer; the observer need make no overt response.

Bandura (1965a) defines a vicarious learning event as ". . . one in which new responses are acquired or the characteristics of existing response repertoires are modified as a function of observing the behavior of others and its reinforcing consequences, without the modeled responses being overtly performed during the exposure period by the viewer" (p. 3). Such a notion also includes the elimination (extinction) or suppression of responses. Imitation, an earlier name for observational learning, has long been recognized to be a by-product of grouping. What is perhaps most puzzling is that so much contention has arisen around the concept of imitation. Most early writers on social behavior mentioned imitation. McDougall (1908), author of the first book bearing the title *Social Psychology* produced by a psychologist, was one authority who proposed that humans had an imitation instinct. The instinct doctrine, in the sense in which it was once used and applied to human behavior, eventually fell into just disrepute. Unfortunately, many phenomena became unpopular topics of study simply because they had been associated with some portion of the doctrine (see Bandura, 1965a). Certainly there is great survival value attached to learning by observing others and their rewards. If one's companion dies after consuming the "deadly nightshade," it is not necessary to sample it oneself and be similarly rewarded in order to learn. The survivor-observer in this case is more likely to bear progeny, but it does not follow that the consequence is a population holding an appropriate instinct.

In addition, learning theory was in its "classic phase" during the early part of this century, and was primarily concerned with classical and instrumental conditioning. Thus it could not easily be adapted to the complex processes that presumably underlie social learning. However, the transition was soon attempted, and one ingenious analysis is that of Miller and Dollard (1941). These authors were primarily aiming at refuting the notion of innately determined imitations. They pointed out that imitation learning was instrumental learning and could be taught to subjects, both animal and human, by a suitable schedule of response-reinforcement contingencies associated with either the target person stimulus or the respondent, or both. Miller and Dollard demonstrated that if subjects were rewarded for matching the responses of target persons, who in turn were rewarded for learning a discrimination problem not observed by the follower subjects, then the follower subject learned to imitate the target subject. Moreover, such "matched-dependent behavior," as it was called, generalized to new situations, new behaviors, and new target subjects. There is little doubt that some imitative behavior can be learned in this way. But, as Bandura (1965a) has pointed out, such a learning situation represents only a special case of discrimination learning; the target person is in effect only a discriminative stimulus. Is it necessary that the observer make a response "stimulated" in some way by the model in order for learning to take place?

Two general kinds of observational learning processes in the presence of the model need to be distinguished:

a)   The observer sees the consequences of the model's behavior; he learns that the behavior leads to such and such. That a sequence of actions leads to a certain reward or punishment is evident to an audience of children when a teacher praises or reproves a child in front of a class.

b)   The observer is directly rewarded or punished for behaving in the way the model behaves. The daughter who attempts to do as her mother does in performing some household chore, and receives praise for doing so, provides an example of the second sort of observational learning. It is this latter form of matching behavior that Miller and Dollard (1941) emphasized.

A number of important theoretical issues in learning theory are raised in the analysis of the vicarious events we have been considering. Some theorists have pondered over what is learned and how it is learned, but we will not discuss these matters in detail here. However, we might mention in passing an important distinction drawn by Bandura (1965a): "... the *acquisition* of matching responses results primarily from stimulus contiguity and associated symbolic processes, whereas reinforcing consequences to the model or to the observer have a major influence on the *performance* of imitatively learned responses" (p. 7). In support of this notion, Bandura (1965b) conducted an experiment in which children observed a filmed sequence of a model displaying strongly aggressive behavior, both verbal and physical; in one condition the model was praised, in another the model was punished, and in a third the model received neither reward nor punishment. After the film, the children were tested for the behavior just observed. That the different audiences had learned different things seemed to be evident from the fact that the subjects in the "model-rewarded" condition gave, on the average, more "imitative responses" than those in the "model-punished" condition, with the no-reinforcement condition falling in between. However, when subjects in all conditions were offered substantial positive reinforcement if they performed the modeled behavior well, average performance in *all* conditions was greatly increased, and the differences among conditions became negligible.

Again we see the importance of distinguishing between learning and performance. Of course, it is obvious that learning is necessarily inferred from behavior or performance, but the experimental disentanglement is not always easily accomplished, especially in social situations.

The vicarious instigation of behavior. We shall consider only one more class of vicarious events of a distinctly social nature: the case where the behavior of the other persons serves as a *cue* or *instigator* in the production of already well-learned behavior. Thus a model may symbolize to the observer the sort of behavior that is approved in a certain type of situation. In other words, models can illustrate or indicate the social norms applicable within the social context in which the observer finds himself. (Social norms are considered here to be cognitions about what behavior is *expected,* along with the *limits* for tolerable behavior deviating from this expectation.) On the other hand, observation of others may arouse responses ordinarily too weak to be given in the particular setting. Obviously, there are a number of important behavioral possibilities, but we shall consider only one example, one that is both well worked out experimentally and highly relevant to interpersonal behavior in general: aggression.

Although aggression is an important concept in the study of individual personality, its definition is essentially social. One is ordinarily not considered to be aggressive toward inanimate objects. However, the most general definition of aggression has it that the goal of the behavior to be called aggressive is to hurt some person *or* thing. Considering only the first class of goal objects, we shall discuss how the mere observation of aggression in others produces an increased probability of an aggressive response in the observer. If the aggression-filled behavioral sequence observed does not directly affect the observer, or if aggressive tendencies are not already present in the observer, there is no reason to expect the aggressive behavior to occur after observation of violence or symbolic punishment executed by a model.

Berkowitz (Berkowitz, 1965; Berkowitz and Geen, 1966; Berkowitz and Rawlings, 1963) has studied the instigation of aggressive behavior experimentally. The basic experimental setup is one where a student subject is either insulted by the experimenter's accomplice upon arriving at the laboratory, or is treated in a neutral fashion. Subsequently, some subjects witness a brutal prizefight scene from the movie *Champion* in which one fighter sustains a savage beating. Other subjects watch a "neutral" film containing no aggression. All subjects are subsequently given the opportunity, under the guise of aiding the experimenter, to administer painful shocks to the accomplice who originally either insulted them or did nothing to them. For some subjects the accomplice is associated with the fight scene in some way (represented as a college boxer, given a name similar to the film character, etc.), and for the others he is not connected with the film sequence at all. The evidence suggests that the initially angered subjects were affected by the film in such a way that they administered greater punishment to the accomplice when he was associated in some way with the boxer role than when he was associated with a neutral role (e.g., speech major).

Boxer-confederates also tended to receive greater shock than speech-confederates, regardless of whether the subject administering the shock was previously angered or not. However, subsequent experiments by Berkowitz and his associates have shown that there is a strong tendency for angered and film-aroused subjects to deal more harshly with confederates who can in some way be associated with the film—and often the association is rather remote.

A number of other interesting results are available, but these examples provide sufficient illustration of the notion that the actions of others, not directly connected with the observer, can exert substantial control over his aggressive responses and can do so in a fairly predictable fashion. Apparently, the members of the audience are not only aroused by what they see, but their latent tendencies can also be *guided* by their experience, whether they are aware of it or not. The persistence of stimulated-aggression effects has not yet been determined. It is fairly common in laboratory experiments for the behavior sampled to span a rather short period of time. One must consequently be cautious about generalizing from these studies to the current and obviously quite important question of how film and television portrayals of violence affect the subsequent behavior of children and other audiences. Berkowitz (1964) has, in fact, discussed this very point at some length.

It is not always clear whether the subject's aggressive behavior following a violent film sequence has resulted from general arousal, disinhibition of preexisting responses, or actual response elicitation of some sort. In some cases a subtle indication may be transmitted as to what general practical behavior is acceptable or expected under the circumstances. These are important questions deserving an answer (see Berkowitz, 1962, 1965;

Bandura and Walters, 1963; Walters and Parke, 1964). However, it is sufficient for our purposes to realize that the simple grouping of persons involves a number of complex psychological processes, and that these are not so mysterious that "group mind' or "herd instincts" need be entertained as explanatory concepts. The processes we have just discussed might be considered as extensions of the continuum that we have been pursuing since our introductory discussion of passive-audience effects. We have not yet passed the point at which one might reasonably begin to describe the "together situation" as clearly interactive, though it is strongly social. Clearly the audience-actor situation works both ways; an actor is affected by the presence of others, and from the others' point of view the actor produces rather strong effects on those who are passively observing.

While the social settings we have considered so far have to some degree emphasized arousal, elicitation of responses, or information transmission as a by-product, we will now mention briefly a social context that is rather different: namely, social support.

Social Support and the Presence of Others

If the mere presence of others is arousing, can it sometimes also be pleasant, comforting, or supportive? Certainly, it is commonplace to observe that in the face of threat, human children as well as immature animals seek close proximity with the parent, and sometimes with one another (see Harlow and Harlow, 1965). The simpler question that we ask here is: Do threatened persons seek the presence of others, even minimal acquaintances or strangers? If so, why and under what conditions? The widespread belief that unpleasant circumstances increase an individual's desire to be with others is perhaps best expressed by the old saying that "misery loves company." There are, however, two issues involved here: (a) a person's felt need for others when he is under some sort of stress, and (b) the level of actual task performance in the company of others when some stress is present. Though the main thrust of our discussion involves the second question, let us briefly consider the first.

We have been using the term stress in a general way, but suppose that stress refers to the production of some degree of anxiety in the subject. Anxiety is arousing, among other things, and hence the notion we are concerned with here overlaps to some extent with the ideas presented in our earlier discussion of the general term arousal. Schachter (1959) has studied the inclination of subjects to affiliate with others when they are apprehensive about a forthcoming experiment which involves receiving a painful shock. The avoidance of isolation in such a circumstance may be due to the fear of being alone during the painful event. Walters and Parke (1964) have pointed out, in more detail, ". . . that isolation becomes emotionally arousing when (a) it is perceived as a source of danger; or (b) when it functions, in a catalytic manner, to heighten apprehension concerning some forthcoming event; or (c) when it provides an occasion for the recall of some earlier emotionally arousing experience" (p. 260). Being alone, then, can be interpreted as anxiety-provoking, or as serving to exacerbate any anxiety already present.

In an experiment by Schachter (1959), student subjects who were awaiting their turn to participate in an experiment in which they expected to receive painful electric shocks were offered the opportunity to wait either alone or in the presence of others. Schachter observed that a significant proportion of the subjects preferred to wait in the presence of others faced with the *same predicament.* The preference was exhibited even though communication was restricted among those awaiting the common fate. It turned out that the preference for the company of others during stressful anticipation was peculiar to firstborn and only children; later-born children did not show this preference. Wrightsman (1960) essentially confirmed this finding and added that when subjects anticipating shock waited together, less intraindividual variability in reported anxiety was found in persons who were in the company of others than in those who were alone.

The presence of others may serve, or may be imagined to serve, several useful functions, especially if the others are attending to the same anticipated events. Others may provide useful information about how to deal with the forthcoming task. Even noncommunicative others can provide some cues as to proper deportment in the face of threat. Such information can itself reduce the threat of embarrassment through bumbling and of the accompanying derogation by one's peers, who are expected to be present at the forthcoming sesssion. We have only scratched the surface of this important line of inquiry, but it is evident that prior to task performance the subject can use or be influenced by the presence of others, even though the role of the others may not be that of actively comforting the apprehensive individual.

Zajonc (1966) has taken a somewhat similar approach to the presence of others during the *performance of a task* having some associated stress. Thus, Zajonc focuses on the second of the two questions posed at the beginning of this section. He considers experimental data from both animals and human subjects from the point of view of the arousal hypotheses he formulated about the together and alone situations. One of the studies discussed by Zajonc is that of Seidman, Bensen, Miller, and Meeland (1957), in which Army enlisted men were subjected to both a together and an alone condition following basic training. In the alone condition, only the experimenter was present and the subject was to administer increasing levels of electric shock to himself until he had reached the highest level he could tolerate; in the together condition another subject was supposedly (though not actually) yoked to the subject so that both received the shock level that the subject had selected. The maximum shock tolerated in the together condition was substantially higher than that tolerated in the alone condition. Seidman *et al.* concluded that the presence of a partner with whom to "share" the stress greatly aids one's stress tolerance. Zajonc, however, suggests that soldiers following basic training may well work hard to bear excessive pain, for lack of courage is hardly an admirable quality to display to one's comrades. "Sharing adversity" may thus have had little to do with the increased tolerance in the together situation. Whether or not the notion of socially induced arousal is applicable here is also not clear. The point is that the idea of sharing misery or obtaining "social support" need not be evoked to explain "performance enhancement" as observed in social circumstances of the type found in the study by Seidman *et al.*

In a somewhat more cogent study, Ader and Tatum (1963), also using the alone and together conditions, placed subjects in a situation in which they had to learn how to avoid unpleasant electric shocks. However, they were given a minimum of information as to how to deal with the avoidance; in other words, they had to *acquire* an avoidance response. Electrodes were attached to the legs of graduate and medical students seated about a table on which a red button had been mounted. The experimenter left immediately after informing the subjects that they could not detach the electrodes, but without informing them as to the function of the red button. A shock was administered every 10 seconds unless the red button was depressed, in which case shock was delayed for 10 seconds. The avoidance response was learned much more quickly by subjects alone than by subjects in pairs. In fact, only two pairs out of 12 learned the avoidance response, and they required a very much longer time to do so than did the single subjects. Zajonc (1966), in discussing the Ader and Tatum experiment, emphasizes the fact that the subjects "responded at considerably higher rates when in pairs than when alone," but only *after* the avoidance response was well learned.

In summary, we may say that Zajonc has implied that many situations with task-associated stress can be accounted for by the notion of arousal in the presence of others. (He carefully avoids extending his generalizations to the case where subjects are waiting anxiously for a threatening experience, as in the Schachter experiments.) If the situation calls for the emission of a well-learned response, production is facilitated by the presence of others. If new learning is required or information must be processed in a new way, then the presence of an audience or of coactors is inhibiting. Clearly, when interpreting data about stressful situations, we must conclude that the particular task-generated behavior exhibited is a crucial consideration. It may seem that subjects are merely sharing misery or obtaining comfort from others. Similarly, the presence of others may provide substantial information, whether this be clues about the way the forthcoming task is to be approached or cues as to the appropriate behavior to be exhibited.

We should not leave this topic without emphasizing that we have dealt with only a small part of the idea of socially based emotional support. From the standpoint of the task-behavior and the audience-coaction paradigms, it would seem that many of the "social support" effects can be accounted for by processes simpler than those associated with comforting or sharing anxiety with those about to experience something unpleasant. However, as the complexity of the relationship between the subject and the others increases (through friendship, competition, etc.), the subject's attitudes and similar variables must surely become more important.

Concluding Remarks
on Learning from Models and Social Support

The overtly passive observer is indeed strongly affected by the active behavior of others. Although much individual performance appears to be related to observer states, such as arousal, induced by the mere presence of others, it is at the same time evident that the presence of others may serve to provide cues or impart special meanings to the subject; it may even serve as a useful standard for the judging of appropriate social and task behavior. However, it is likewise evident that the nature of the task itself continues to play a crucial role in explaining the effects of others on individual performance. In fact, the role demanded by the particular task, and the behavior it stimulates, becomes an increasingly critical factor as we move from passive through active audiences of various kinds to interaction situations.

The complex role of noninteracting others is well illustrated by a consideration of the social support notion that we discussed earlier. The experiments of Schachter suggested that apparently apprehensive subjects preferred the mere company of others. Of course, we have no evidence that arousal *per se* was thereby reduced. More important, the companions sought were not the *source* of the apprehension. On the other hand, an audience present during task performance may serve a rather different role, and may even occasionally be a source of threat. In fact, Cottrell (1968) has suggested that a necessary condition for the "audience effect" is that the audience be in some sense perceived as a source of positive or negative outcomes. Henchy and Glass (1968) have demonstrated that to the extent that audiences are increasingly presented as evaluators, individual performance accordingly declines. However, they were unable to demonstrate any concomitant change in arousal.

At this point, it is perhaps best to conclude that the kind of audience and the point in time at which it exerts its influence are key considerations in determining the specific effects to be expected in the individual subject. This conclusion is hardly surprising, but it serves to emphasize the need for conceiving of the individual, the task, and the situation (the audience) as interlocking systems, even when the circumstances of task performance are so apparently simple.

CHAPTER THREE

Social Interaction and Performance

INDIVIDUAL PERFORMANCE AND COLLECTIVE PERFORMANCE

The idea of interaction between persons implies simply that the behavior of one person is in turn a stimulus or part of a stimulus complex for the behavior of a second. Some students of social behavior have even proposed that the "interpersonal behavioral event" is the basic datum or unit of social psychology (see Krech, Crutchfield, and Ballachey, 1962). Be that as it may, it seems fair to say that social interaction is ultimately the central concern of social psychology.

Although the notion of interaction suggests reciprocity between or among a set of two or more people, some social exchanges among people may be characterized as *one-way interactions*. In such exchanges the bulk or all of the stimulus to behavior goes in one direction (that is from person *A* to person *B*). In the preceding sections we dealt with some features characteristic of essentially one-way social processes. We will now consider social situations in which a somewhat more obvious kind of exchange takes place among persons who are aware of and who respond to each other to a significant degree. In other words, we are moving further along the continuum running from minimal to maximal social involvement on the part of one or more persons. In essence, we must now consider not only the response of a single person to a task and to the presence of others, but also the complex effects of the *exchange* with other persons.

Although an amazing number of different tasks have been employed in small group research, the qualitative range of behaviors actually elicited by group tasks has been rather limited. Most attention has been devoted to goals or tasks that involve intellective processes rather than motor skills. We shall therefore consider the following two issues before discussing group performance in detail: (a) the general area of "thinking," variously described in the literature as complex processes, higher processes, information processing, and a number of other things; and (b) the problem of analysis and control of the group task-stimulus itself. The study of the interacting group requires that we consider not only the person-task relation, but the person-person relation as well.

The Complex Processes:
Learning-Concept Formation, Problem Solving, and Decision Making

Various tasks provoke varying degrees of abstract behavior in the individual person or set of persons, and may even in practice require some motor performance. But, in essence, thinking is distinguished by a ". . . degree of internal representational, mediational, or symbolic activity" (Bourne and Battig, 1966, p. 541).

Bourne and Battig (1966) further characterize the domain of thinking as follows (pp. 541-542):

> Although thinking is generally considered to be a multistage process, there has been far less than complete agreement as to either the number or the descriptive labels to be applied to the various stages. Principally because of its close correspondence with methodological distinctions, we have chosen to conceptualize thinking as a three-stage process, consisting in (1) a preparatory reception and categorization or organization of information, from either internal or external sources, or *conceptual behavior;* (2) largely on the basis of this information, the development and formulation of various alternative response sequences or courses of action that might be attempted, corresponding to what is generally termed *problem solving;* and (3) the choice or decision as to which of these courses of action is to be followed, to be referred to as *decision making.*

The study of group performance, either in the field or in controlled laboratory work, has not always employed tasks that can be so neatly categorized as *primarily* information acquisition, processing, or execution. In practice, most group tasks are a mixture of these categories. For example, it is difficult to conceive of a task that does not involve some judgmental or decision process, even though the major group effort may be directed toward processing old information in such a way that several solutions or response alternatives can be constructed for final group action. In fact, the definition of just what constitutes a task for a *group* has proved surprisingly troublesome. So often the social psychologist's interest is not in performance *per se,* but in some feature of interpersonal relations. The task serves only to provoke the requisite interaction or to focus the group's attention on itself; group output is strictly secondary. In this book, of course, we consider the group product or goal attainment to be primary, and focus on the internal social processes as mediating the member inputs (individual information or personal proclivities of one sort or another) that eventually result in the group solution or judgment.

Group Tasks:
Questions and Issues of Taxonomy

The confusion surrounding the definition of a group task stems less from an unclear delineation of the behavior to be studied than it does from the inability of the researcher to achieve stimulus control in the same way that it can be achieved in psychophysics and so many other areas of psychology. The group response is itself a compound event, and only some of the components (member task and social responses) may have been identified previously by direct observation or obtained independently of the group output.

There have been, roughly speaking, three approaches to the classification or definition of group tasks:

1.   The *task is treated formally* as a set of elements among which relations of various types can be specified. The persons comprising the group are likewise treated as a set of elements among which various type of relations can be specified. Finally the two systems, task and person, are related to each other (see Oeser and O'Brien, 1967). This formal approach has much to recommend it conceptually, but an empirical demonstration of its utility has yet to appear. The tasks that have been used in group performance research in the past and that will probably be used in the near future are simply not amenable to diagrammatic analysis. Likewise, the measurement difficulties associated with specifying the relations among positions, among persons, and between positions and persons are formidable, especially in informal face-to-face groups.

2.   A second approach involves the *discovery of task dimensions* which actually make an important difference in group work and member relations. Tasks may then be classified or ordered along these dimensions. Shaw (1963) has attempted to scale a large number of tasks that have already been used in some way or have been selected as likely candidates for future use. Such listings are helpful, but they rarely aid the experimenter who seeks to increase his *control* over theoretically important parts of the task.

3.   The third and by far most common approach to the classification of tasks has been *intuitive*. A task or problem is selected for administration to a group because it seems to embody those attributes that the investigator wishes to explore. For example, if the researcher wishes to study the suborganizations that evolve during group deliberations in order to better sustain a cooperative division of labor, he might very well choose a goal that

is physically divisible into rather obvious subtasks. A series of small arithmetic problems the answers to which must be put together in some way to obtain an overall answer affords the opportunity for a socially mediated division of labor which an investigator might choose to study under various experimental conditions. We do not mean to imply that the selection of group tasks is ordinarily capricious. On the contrary, the task is usually carefully analyzed to determine whether the desired variables are operational in its performance (see Roby and Lanzetta, 1958).

In summary, we must still regard the question of a viable taxonomy of group tasks as an open issue. The basic problem has been well-defined in recent years, but it remains unsolved. Much of the discussion dealing with group task taxonomy could have been pursued earlier, during our discussion of noninteractive social contexts. However, this topic fits in here because it is precisely the addition of the person-person relation to the person-task relation that creates the most serious task control problems.

The relationship between group and task. The effects of social interaction on task performance operate on two levels. The first level is the *group* response to the task following interaction; the second is the *individual* responses of members following interaction. In terms of the first level one question that is intuitively intriguing has to do with the information about each member that is available or can be recovered from the group product *alone.* If the group must agree on a single problem solution, elect a single decision alternative, or invent a compromise from initially contending views, the individual task responses are lost. Such a many-to-one (person-task relation) format might be regarded as *information reducing.* That is to say, task responses or solutions of individual members cannot be specified exactly from the group solutions alone (see Posner, 1964). This is not only the most common research format, but it in many ways poses the most challenging questions for both theory and research. A number of existing groups in our culture might be characterized as predominantly information reducing—legislative committees, boards of directors, juries, and others that are required to come up with single answers, decisions, or recommendations. Of course, many formal groups also maintain records or minutes, and these sometimes allow individual or subgroup products to be recovered independently of the group product itself.

An *information-conserving* format yields group output that preserves the individual contributions of members. The group product consists of the indentifiable solutions of all the members. To be sure, a member's opinion or solution might change as a consequence of the discussion, but there is no final group-mediated combination that "loses" the individual contribution, whatever it turns out to be. A common way of using this format is to observe pre- and post-discussion decisions or solutions by individuals in order not only to determine something about how the subject was affected in the interim but also to infer something about the nature of the discussion.

Locus of task definition. Some tasks could reasonably be presented either to individuals or to a group. A word puzzle, for example, presents a challenge to an individual person as well as to a set of persons who cooperate in its solution. This type of task is defined in terms of individuals but the definition remains applicable to groups as well. On the other hand, a number of tasks are impossible, or undefined, for individual persons apart from a group. For example, the major chore facing a group may be reaching agreement on some political issue. An individual subject may have no doubts as to his own position, but be distressed to find others in disagreement. The resolution of this disagreement in order to achieve consensus may represent a formidable task for the group, but there is no counterpart to this task for the isolated individual.

Thus tasks may be defined in terms of individuals only, groups only, or both individuals and groups. Obviously, such distinctions are likely in practice to be a matter of degree. However, as we shall see, much of the confusion surrounding theoretical explanations of group performance is traceable to a lack of specificity as to what constitutes the group task, how group structure and problem structure match, and how task elements may be varied systematically after the fashion of traditional stimulus control.

Continuous-response tasks and feedback. We shall make one final distinction concerning group tasks. Up to this point we have implied that our interest in the group's activities ends with the production of some solution or decision. Yet it is obvious that for many important situations group interaction can result in a number of products perhaps distributed in time or over particular occasions. Moreover, there may be some sort of payoff or reinforcement associated with such a sequence of responses or products. The nature of the payoff, in fact, may constitute the dominant force in determining the form of interpersonal relations associated with the group effort. Just as rewards and punishments tend to aid in shaping the behavior of the individual organism, so may the group's response rate and quality fluctuate with the nature of the feedback or schedule of reinforcement. For example, group cooperation, morale, and cohesiveness usually increase with task success and decrease with failure.

The number of response alternatives allowed or provoked by a task and the nature of the feedback contained in the task system have a significance for groups that is not evident in the case of individual task performance. The existence of several task-response alternatives, especially when they are associated with different rewards, permits and even encourages conflict, competition, or sharing. In fact, we shall conclude our discussion of group task considerations by briefly considering a class of tasks that has as an essential defining characteristic a particular interpersonal relationship: cooperation-competition. This dimension is distinctly social in that the "problem" as such might not even exist without the presence of another person. Similarly, there might be no possibility of overcoming an obstacle or obtaining something without the aid of another person.

There are a number of ways in which cooperative and competitive task behavior may be cast for study, but one way has proved to be very helpful: describing the task-payoff-person system in terms of *game theory*. This term is perhaps unfortunate in that "game" bears a frivolous connotation. On the other hand, parlor and playground games do bear a resemblance to a number of actual business situations and other confrontations of a highly serious sort. Informally, the "essence of a 'game' in this context is that it involves decision makers with different goals or objectives whose fates are intertwined" (Shubik, 1964, p. 8).

Game theory. The social importance of what we call game theory may be clarified if we consider Schelling's (1958) classification of two-person game situations: (a) pure-coordination situations; (b) pure-conflict situations; and (c) mixed-motive situations. Of course, there are many other classifications of game situations depending on number of persons involved, available strategies, static or dynamic nature of the situation, and so on. For simplicity, we shall consider here *only two-person games.*

A *pure-coordination situation* is one where the interests of participants coincide; a "solution" exists in that there is a mutual response or decision pattern among strategies that maximizes payoffs for everyone. The achievement of coordinated actions is usually a problem only when the alternatives to be chosen are not immediately visible to the players, or when the participants are not in a face-to-face relation. In any event, such situations are fundamentally task setups in which "nature" or some encumbering set of circumstances is a large part of the difficulty to be overcome.

A *pure-conflict situation* (sometimes called a zero-sum game) is the other extreme. In this situation the personal choice of strategies represents an attempt to compete with the other player for limited resources. One player's gain is the other's loss. That is, the amount player A wins is the amount player B loses. (Some *n-person* zero-sum games are not pure-conflict contests, but we shall not consider these cases now.) In essence the resolution of this competition is the resolution of the task itself.

A *mixed-motive situation* is one in which no outcome, no set of strategy choices, guarantees a maximum payoff to all participants. There exists the opportunity for maximizing one's own gain, but at the same time the "motive" for cooperation is also present in that both participants may achieve something by coordinating their play. (Both the mixed-motive and pure-coordination games are non-zero-sum games, since in each the amount gained by one player is not necessarily the amount lost by the other.)

A number of circumstances that appear to have little in common with the game situation may profitably be interpreted in terms of game theory, especially if interest is focused on the *outcomes* of interaction. Such circumstances include the phenomenon of an apparently cooperative group turning into a competitive one. Also, within the larger group, subgroups sometimes seem to develop local interpersonal conflicts, even though the group as a whole is essentially cooperative in nature. Thus the pure-coordination task changes into a pure-conflict situation, despite the fact that the task itself does not imply any sort of conflict. Indeed the behavior of most task-oriented groups over time is probably best described as a mixture of conflict and cooperation

In summary, some tasks exist by virtue of the fact that something must or may be gained by working *with* one or more other persons. Other tasks exist by virtue of the fact that what is to be gained must be obtained *from* one or more others. Still other tasks are mixtures. It is probably true that many goal-striving groups contain dyads (two-person units) or larger subgroups that are constructing conflict or mixed-motive "games" within the context of the larger group, which may be working cooperatively at the overall task. In fact the overall task may lack a game-like quality *per se*. This complexity of interaction modes has led a number of social psychologists to simplify the interpersonal processes to be studied by focusing on experimental situations in which two persons confront each other in the ways we have described above (for example, see Kelley, 1968). The important feature of such dyadic interactions is that the resolution of the interdependency problem is at the same time a task solution that conveys rewards and costs to the participants. (Gergen, 1969, deals with these social-task exchange processes at some length, and hence we will not consider them further.)

INDIVIDUALS VERSUS GROUPS

We shall consider initially the simple contrast between individual and group performance. There are several reasons for making this apparently simple comparison. First of all, the individual-group paradigm allows us to complete the orderly progression we started earlier with passive audience effects on performance. The progression also reflects a historical trend in social psychology, and discussing this trend permits us to show how the initially simple problem of individual-group contrast grew from merely demonstrating a productivity "difference" to an appreciation of the complexity of group processes. The determination of whether group or individual work is more efficient or satisfying under various task and environmental conditions remains an important practical problem having implications for groups varying from industrial work settings to political institutions. However, we shall take the position that the more important goal is to determine how individuals "turn into groups." More specifically, we seek to discover how a set of disparate individuals arrange or *combine* their several task and personal predilections through social interaction. The attempt to answer the original question of whether groups or individuals were superior performers (were faster, more accurate, made fewer errors, etc.) has thus expanded into a search for the variables involved in group processes *per se.*

Learning

The relative emphasis on learning, problem-solving, and decision-making groups has been uneven. More attention has been devoted to problem-solving groups than to groups facing learning or decision tasks. Surprisingly little is known about how groups acquire and store information. However, many data are available from several applied settings, such as the classroom, in which class (group) discussion is pitted against individual work on some measure of retention. The results of such studies are quite mixed, possibly because of the wide range of task and dependent variables involved, but usually the individual-group differences are not great. On the whole, it seems that group methods are less important for producing content mastery or knowledge differences than in bringing about favorable changes in personality and social adjustment. Of course, these latter gains are not negligible and are important in their own right.

From the limited experimental data on group learning it appears that when a group-individual difference exists at all, groups tend to make fewer errors, and sometimes reach the learning criterion in a shorter time. For example, experiments by Gurnee (1937, 1939) generally confirm group superiority in maze learning. The maze used by Gurnee was composed of pairs of bolt heads with a pointer attached which could be swung from one bolt to the other in such a way that a light came on when the setting was correct. The maze was solved when the sequence could be correctly executed. Groups were required to vote on the correct response at each step and, like individuals, to focus on the elimination of errors during the six trials they were allotted (Gurnee, 1937). Groups in general made fewer errors and completed the first perfect trial sooner. However, when a seventh trial was administered to all subjects as individuals, there was no detectable difference between individuals and group-experienced subjects. In the 1939 experiment, Gurnee essentially repeated the bolt-maze study and also required a six-trial learning sequence for pairs of digits. This time, the seventh trial (all subjects were tested as individuals) revealed that the group-experienced subjects were also superior in that they made fewer errors. However, mazes, or other mechanical apparatus that permits visual display of responses, allow group members to exploit *observational learning* opportunities in addition to any benefits from discussion.

In an experiment by Perlmutter and de Montmollin (1952), 20 three-person groups were required to learn two-syllable nonsense words. One list was learned by individuals alone, but in the presence of the other two; a second list was learned by the group as a cooperative project. Half the subjects worked first as individuals and half worked first as members of an interacting group. Thus two kinds of groups and two kinds of individual

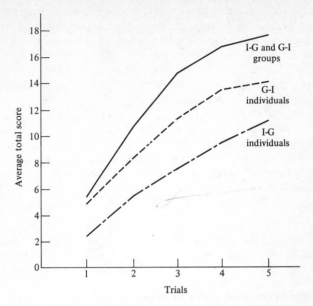

Fig. 3.1 The comparison of average individual and group learning for each of five trials. (From Perlmutter and de Montmollin, 1952. Copyright 1952 by the American Psychological Association, and reproduced by permission.)

subjects were generated by the pre- and post-testing experience. Group experience improved subsequent individual performance, but previous individual experience failed to provide an enhancement of group performance. However, the main comparison from our point of view revealed that the two kinds of groups were both significantly superior to individual subjects from both of the individual conditions. The course of group and individual learning is shown in Fig. 3.1 (where "I-G" stands for the individual-group sequence and "G-I" for the reverse sequence).

If we were to summarize the individual-group learning experiments, which we have only sampled here, the most fitting generalization would be that although the difference between individuals and groups is frequently negligible, any significant discrepancy almost uniformly favors groups. Groups are more likely than individuals to come up with a correct response; they make fewer errors; and frequently they arrive earlier at a response or learning criterion.

Problem Solving

The range of problem types is very great, and a variety of experimental settings is evident in the literature on group problem solving. However, here again we may pose the same simple contrast of group with individual, but now the task is a problem to be solved. The overall conclusion is that groups are usually superior to individuals in the proportion of correct solutions (quality) and number of errors, but somewhat less often are groups superior in terms of time required to reach an answer. Although we obviously would expect somewhat different relationships from some kinds of tasks and groups, the preceding summary statement holds over a fairly wide range of cases (Lorge, Fox, Davitz, and Brenner, 1958).

A typical early study is the classic work of Marjorie Shaw (1932) in which both isolated individuals and four-person groups solved complex intellectual puzzles requiring several steps to be taken to reach a correct answer. In the first part of the experiment, subjects were given three similar puzzles each having a unique, self-confirming answer when that answer was attained (these are called "eureka" puzzles by Lorge *et al.,* 1958). One of these "eureka problems," known from antiquity as the Tartaglia, was as follows:

> Three Missionaries and three Cannibals are on the *A*-side of the river. Get them across to the *B*-side by means of a boat which holds only two at one time. All the Missionaries and one Cannibal can row. Never under any circumstances or at any time may the Missionaries be outnumbered by the Cannibals.

In the second session, the three problems had a less insightful answer and involved rearranging words to complete a prose passage, rearranging words to complete the last lines of a sonnet, and finding the minimum-mileage route for a schoolbus with a given capacity to pick up children at a certain number of stops. For the combined data on all problems, Shaw found that the proportion of solutions by groups was higher than that for individuals. Unlike so many previous studies, Shaw carefully observed the working groups and attempted to analyze the nature of the social interaction taking place during the solution. This tactic represented a substantial methodological advance for the time, though such ancillary data are routinely collected in many studies today. In explaining the reasons for the group superiority, Shaw used the following social observations: (a) groups seem to check errors and reject incorrect solutions; (b) another member rejects an incorrect solution more often than the person proposing the suggested solution; and (c) when errors are made, individuals tend to err sooner in the process of solution than do groups. Shaw also observed that all members of groups do not cooperate or participate to the same degree in solving problems.

Thorndike (1938) suspected that problems allowing a wide range of acceptable answers might favor groups more than individuals. Using three tasks in which there was either a wide or a restricted range of allowable answers, he found that indeed group superiority was greater with problems which allowed a greater variety of possible responses.

If attention is focused on the time required for completion rather than on the proportion of acceptable answers, the same group superiority is observed. However, as Taylor and Faust (1952) discovered, the saving in

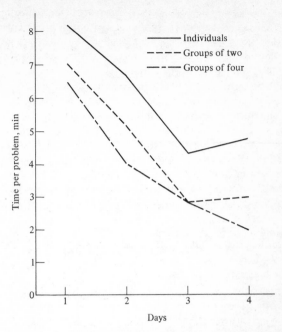

Fig. 3.2 Time per problem for groups of two and four and for individual subjects on each of four days of work. (From Taylor and Faust, 1952. Copyright 1952 by the American Psychological Association, and reproduced by permission.)

man-hours suggests that the question of *relative efficiency* is not negligible in the comparison of experimental groups with individuals. Taylor and Faust required individuals, two-person, and four-person cooperating groups to guess topics in the game of Twenty Questions on each of several days. Results were recorded in terms of the number of questions per problem, number of failures, and time required. The results for solution time are recorded in Fig. 3.2.

The study by Taylor and Faust was addressed to a number of issues, but the major conclusions may be summarized as follows (Taylor and Faust, 1952, p. 366):

> ... group performances were superior to individual performance in terms of number of questions, number of failures, and elapsed time per problem; but the performance of groups of four was not superior to that of groups of two, except in terms of the number of failures to reach solution. The performance of individuals was superior to that of either size group in terms of number of man-minutes required for solution.

The last finding introduces an important concept into the individual-group question: the productivity per unit time per person. Actually, Husband

(1940) had earlier posed a similar question about efficiency while discovering, among other things, that pairs surpassed individuals on several kinds of tasks; but the superiority was especially marked for decoding and jig-saw puzzles, while more routine tasks (arithmetic problems) did not reveal significant individual-group differences.

It would be easy to write off the question of efficiency as simply a matter of cost-accounting or as an application having relatively little to do with a fundamental understanding of group processes. However, we shall see that taking into account the group's apparent resources opens up an extremely important approach to the study of group performance. Obviously, the major group advantage is that more than one head is available for storing information, if learning is emphasized by the task, or providing already stored information, if the task primarily requires recall.

In other words, the group potentially can increase performance through *redundancy*. That is to say, if the problem requires that everyone work at the same thing and if individual performance is to some degree unreliable (i.e., some probability of error exists), then multiperson work by means of duplication provides a check on the quality of the group's output. If each person possesses unique but relevant information, and the task requires the several pieces of information, then the pooling of this information will allow groups potentially to solve problems that an individual *cannot* attack successfully.

Moreover, if the task may be broken into subproblems, then different group members may *simultaneously* work at different portions of the task. This strategy accelerates work and allows early responders to check the work of the slower persons. In quite a different way, questioning and debating during social interaction may *stimulate* new or different intra-individual thought processes that the uniform environment of the isolated individual might not provide; thus other persons have a cue value in provoking new task approaches. Finally, the mere presence of others (as indicated earlier) is known to be motivating, and thus is an advantage for some tasks. Moreover, groups mediate a number of appealing by-products, ranging from status to plain fun, that have nothing to do with task performance, but which serve to keep one working.

On the other hand, arousal can be too strong, and as documented earlier, some tasks are particularly difficult when the individual member of a group is aroused. An additional grouping disadvantage, well known to examination-taking students, is the outright distraction from other persons engaged in some activity that competes with one's own thoughts. Interpersonal exchanges, either involving others or involving the respondent, must be scheduled or coordinated to be useful; and therein lies the crux of the matter. Effective group performance apparently requires that member efforts be *organized* or *structured* to maximize the potential advantages of collective resources. Recall that we have been considering primarily groups that are free to organize themselves or reach a product in any way they choose. Such groups are the simplest to understand, are likely to reveal the formulation of a social process or organizational scheme in a forthright way, and are the most frequently studied sort of group.

Although we might judge the performance of any sort of subject by comparing him to some criterion, it is not so easy to judge the effectiveness of social processes within even a very small group. The reason for this is that the direct assessment of social response patterns, the tallying of discussion content, and the characterization of nonverbal stimuli consitute a formidable task, even when a number of experienced judges are available as "measuring instruments." We shall return to this important problem of measuring and representing social processes in later sections. However, the problem of a criterion or standard against which to judge group performance remains an important issue, for we should like to answer the question of whether or not a group achieves the optimal coordination of resources under this or that set of conditions. If optimal performance is not achieved, why is this so? In general, when (and under what conditions) are "two heads better than one"? And when do "too many cooks spoil the broth"—and why?

Decision Making and Simple Judgments

One approach, potentially useful in resolving some of the questions posed in the previous section, arose in the 1920's at an early point in the study of *group decisions*—actually simple judgments in which subjects made estimates of stimulus numerosity, size, temperature, or the like. Unfortunately, the potential theoretical value of this approach was imperfectly recognized at that time. To illustrate, let us consider the early experiments of Knight who in one of her studies (1921) required students to estimate privately the temperature of the classroom. The estimates fluctuated widely, ranging from 60° to 80°. The true temperature was 72°. Knight then created a "group" by averaging the individual estimates herself. The mean of this "staticized" group was 72.4°. Was this a bona fide grouping effect, or was it an empirical demonstration of statistical sampling theory?

Gordon (1923) in a rather similar study required students to rank a set of weights, and then correlated the obtained orderings against the true order. The average correlation was .41. Next Gordon set up "staticized" groups of 5, 10, 20, and 50 by randomly grouping the individual subjects' judgments into collections of 5, 10, 20, and 50 and taking the average of the "members' " rankings as the group's judgment. For staticized groups of five the overall average correlation with the actual weight order was .68, and for groups of 50 it was .94. Gordon's conclusion was that a superiority of grouping over individual effort was thereby demonstrated. (Remember, no *actual group* judgments were obtained at all!) A large number of experiments using several different tasks, but essentially the same approach, have tended to obtain approximately the same results.

Stroop (1932) repeated the Gordon experiment but required *each* of the subjects to make many judgments. Thus he combined 5, 10, 20, and 50 judgments of the *same person*, as opposed to several judgments from different persons, and achieved virtually the same results as did Gordon. That is to say, the average of many judgments by an individual correlated better with the true value than did single judgments. Stroop pointed out that the superiority of group performance was not so much at issue in Knight's and Gordon's use of staticized groups as was a demonstration of how error variance can be reduced. As is well known, the reliability of a test of imperfectly measuring items may be increased by the addition of similar items. In other terms, the standard error of the mean is smaller than the standard deviation of a random variable for all samples larger than one. [A clear and sophisticated explication of this judgment problem is available in a discussion by Zajonc (1962).]

To be sure, we have considered very simple decisions in this section, and the conditions of producing a response have been socially rather barren. Nevertheless, the issue of staticized groups (also called nominal or concocted groups) has suggested an important new approach to research on group performance. For several years the label "statistical artifact" was attached to the use of these statistical pooling notions in individual-group comparisons, and this label, along with the fact that such "groups" never actually met or existed at all, resulted in a relative neglect of their potential. Moreover, the implications of the judgment pooling notion (with regard to *both* theory and experiment) were almost totally ignored in the more complex areas of decision making and problem solving.

In the last three sections we have considered the comparison of individuals with groups working at three classes of tasks: information acquisition, information processing, and decision making. In this third section, we have introduced a new idea, or rather a new question. That question has to do with the very basis of comparison between individuals and groups. Even though we were concerned with the question of efficiency *per se*, it turned out that some sort of *baseline* was required for us to evaluate accurately the group's performance. The important point is that, by pooling or combining individual performance under various hypothetical arrangements, we can better judge not only what groups *might do* to achieve optimal performance, but also what actual groups *might have done*. At least the direction of deviation from the hypothetical baseline gives us some clue about the way social interaction may have treated individual proposals. We shall consistently emphasize this theme in subsequent discussions.

In recent years the complexities surrounding the comparison of individual and group products have come to be more thoroughly appreciated. The individual-group comparison is now coming to be regarded as a special case of the more important question of how individual products are combined into a group product through the interaction of the members.

INDIVIDUALS INTO GROUPS

If we were to summarize the comparison of group and individual products, the gross conclusion would be that on most criteria groups *are* generally superior to individuals but that the existence and degree of superiority depend on a number of situational and task factors (see Lorge *et al.*, 1958). If the emphasis is on achieving a *correct* or *good* or *early* answer, then a group has a higher probability of achieving this aim (other things being equal) than does the single individual. In practice, no experimenter or other higher authority is available to judge the relative efficiency by *combining* available isolated member responses into some "staticized" group product.

Moreover, many tasks have no obvious logical success or product-ordering criterion. The "correct" response is whatever action the group *can* agree upon as desirable, and the group is a larger sample (and hence a more stable estimate) of the population preference than is the single individual. In other words, if errors are costly relative to success, or if the aim is the preservation of social stability, and man-hours are cheap, then the group affords substantial advantages with regard to task performance quite aside from any extra-task advantages such as pleasure in group discussion or social support.

Theoretical Baselines

Ignoring efficiency of performance *per se*, we might still retain the idea of staticized or concocted group products *theoretically* produced from assumptions about internal group processes. The idea is to construct baselines against which real group performance may be compared (see Davis, 1961, 1969; Davis and Restle, 1963; Zajonc, 1962). Given individual responses or products X, and that social interaction is of the sort Y, then the group product should be Z. Real group performance is then compared with the baseline prediction, Z. If group performance is greater than Z, then hypotheses about social interaction effects for all cases less than Z can be disregarded, and attention focused on obtaining theoretical statements that predict greater than Z. In other words, by observing how real groups deviate from baseline predictions generated by a hypothetical social process, we can exclude all of those other hypotheses that would make the deviation more extreme. We would obviously choose to concentrate on social combination hypotheses that make predictions closer to the level of group performance actually observed. The value of the baseline notion lies in the fact that the direct observation of social behavior, as we have said, is often inordinately difficult or even impossible in some cases.

In essence, the baseline idea is no more than a case for normative theory development in lieu of being able to construct directly an adequate descriptive theory. An adequate theory of group performance for some situation can thus be approached more swiftly by successive approxima-tions. [For a similar idea, see Platt's (1964) discussion of *strong inference.*]

As we have described baselines, these are *social combination schemes* for translating member contributions to the task into a group product. One such scheme is identifiable as an average, as in Stroop's discussion of group judgments; but other schemes are possible, and even necessary, to deal with other kinds of groups. Moreover, the study of even a simple judgment-averaging scheme can sometimes lead to rather surprising conclusions. For example, Zajonc (1966, pp. 101-102) has pointed out:

> Combined individual judgments will surpass individual judgments *only* if a majority of the individuals making judgments have a fair chance of being correct. To put it differently, if most of the correlations between individual orders [of a set of rankings] and the true order are positive, then Gordon's conclusion holds. If, however, the correlations are negative, . . . then the combined judgments will be worse than those of single individuals.

The conclusion can be demonstrated by rather simple, but apparently not very obvious, arithmetic. The important point is that *both* the social combination scheme and the nature of the individual member *input* determine the nature of the group product.

Problem solving represents a more complex process for a set of persons than do simple judgments, and this may explain why pooling known individual accomplishments to form a baseline was comparatively slow in being applied in this area. In 1954 Taylor proposed that one might assume, for an individual chosen from some population, that there exists a probability of his solving a problem under some set of conditions. If one assumes further that each person in a group behaves independently of the others and is unaffected (positively or negatively) by discussion, then it is possible to calculate the probability that the group will contain at least one solver. For many kinds of problems (e.g., eureka problems), the group may be assumed to solve the problem if at least one member does so. Although such a chain of assumptions may be dubious in practice, the Taylor model does provide a kind of "null hypothesis" or baseline that will aid in determining whether the group discussion had an effect on performance, and if so, in which direction the effect was exerted.

Lorge and Solomon (1955) independently advanced the same model as Taylor had proposed, and this was formalized as Model A:

$$P_G = 1 - (1 - P_I)^r,$$

where P_G is the probability that a group will solve the problem, P_I is the probability that an individual will solve it, and r is the size of the group. Model A is one possible mathematical expression of the social interaction assumption of the preceding paragraph. Lorge and Solomon reanalyzed that part of the Shaw experiment (discussed earlier) dealing with eureka problems by comparing their combinatorial scheme (predictions from Model A above) with the group data. They found that the model accounted for two of the three problems, but that the remaining problem required a second model (Model B). This second model hypothesized that pooling (Model A) occurred at each of several independent steps or stages in the problem. Whereas the Shaw experiment had implied the superiority of group performance, the Lorge and Solomon theory now provided a rather simple explanation and one that placed less value on the contribution of discussion. The importance of theory, even when it is advanced to be disproved, is clearly demonstrated by these results.

Obviously there is a wide range of possible schemes for pooling member contributions, other than those advanced by Taylor and by Lorge and Solomon. Before considering these other baselines, as well as attempts at descriptive models of group performance, we might briefly inquire further about the efficiency of group performance relative to individual performance. Two studies will illustrate the general character of the conclusions, one dealing with problem solving and the other with learning. Faust (1959), in a study with four-person *ad hoc* groups and individuals, used both a problem presented in diagram form and a set of three anagrams. The results were in line with what we have come to expect; groups were superior to individuals, but not superior to concocted groups (constructed in this case "by hand" rather than by the Lorge-Solomon equations) composed of "members" who never interacted together. Similar results are available from Anderson (1961), Watson (1928), Marquart (1955), and a number of other studies of group problem solving.

Since a rather simple pooling hypothesis concerning individual products has been at least *sufficient* to explain much of the apparent superiority of groups in judging and problem-solving tasks, it is important to consider the third kind of task, that which emphasizes learning. Recall the experiment by Perlmutter and de Montmollin (1952), described earlier at some length. Their group learning curves for nonsense words were initially at a higher level than individual learning curves, and remained at a higher level throughout the five learning trials. Hoppe (1962), who was interested in the same portion of the Perlmutter-de Montmollin results that we are, was able to adapt Lorge and Solomon's Model A to recall. Subsequently he was able to predict, from the independent mean rate of individual recall, the mean recall for r-person groups trial by trial. The adaptation took the form of an additional assumption (p. 65):

> . . . each of the words in the list has an equal probability of being remembered. Making this assumption the proportion of the entire list recalled by the group, p_{tg}, can be estimated from the proportion of the entire list recalled by individuals, p_{ti}, by the following formula: $p_{tg} = 1 - (1 - p_{ti})^r$. It follows that the predicted group mean, G, is found by multiplying p_{tg} by the number of words on the list.

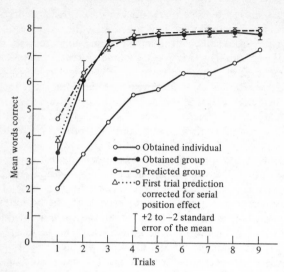

Fig. 3.3 Group and individual learning curves and predictions from a modified version of the Lorge and Solomon Model A. (From Hoppe, 1962. Copyright 1962 by the American Psychological Association, and reproduced by permission.)

Hoppe then performed an experiment contrasting the mean recall of three-person groups with that of individuals. Groups were not allowed recording devices or other aids, *or to divide the task into subtasks*. As is usual in such experiments, cooperative effort was encouraged, but any other sort of social interaction was left to the discretion of the group. Group and individual recall results are given in Fig. 3.3, along with predicted means on each trial. In a second experiment, Hoppe (1967) employed a task emphasizing *both* learning and problem solving, and found that Lorge and Solomon's Models A and B either adequately accounted for, or *overpredicted,* the group response to a significant degree.

It would appear, then, that some form of a simple pooling hypothesis accounts for a surprising amount of group performance in decision making, problem solving, and learning, or perhaps more frequently *overpredicts* group performance. To be sure, the typical laboratory group is composed of strangers, and is ordinarily confronted with relatively simple and logically coherent tasks. Would the results be different if the groups were experienced to some degree, or if they faced a complex task, perhaps calling for more "creative" thinking? One final study might be added to those we have sampled in order to answer this question.

Taylor, Berry, and Block (1958) studied both individuals and groups composed of subjects who had previously had some experience of working together during the course of a semester. The kind of problem administered did not possess a single logically correct answer, but rather was open-end Answers were judged as to quality, and the time required to produce the was also recorded. Prior to the experiment all subjects received a lecture concerning creative thinking, with special emphasis on "brainstorming." Brainstorming, a popular technique introduced by Osborn (1957), has been widely thought to improve task-oriented group performances. The aim of brainstorming is to dispel the social restraint experienced by a group member. Such "restraint" might arise as a bar to productive and creative performance on an assigned problem. In essence, brainstorming requires that criticism of ideas be ruled out, and that freewheeling or wild ideas be considered worthy of discussion; quantity of ideas is a welcome goal, but improvement on and recombination of old ideas are also encouraged. Taylor *et al.* randomly concocted groups from among individuals who had worked alone, and compared the concocted group results with products from real four-person groups. The findings were quite clear. Real groups were distinctly inferior to concocted groups on (a) mean total number of ideas produced, (b) mean number of unique ideas produced, and (c) three different measures that weighted in different ways the quality of ideas produced. The Taylor *et al.* results have subsequently been confirmed by others (e.g., Dunnette, Campbell, and Jaastad, 1963), although one study (Parnes and Meadow, 1959) has led to the conclusion that groups receiving brainstorming instructions possess distinct advantages.

In summary, we might conclude that the direct performance advantage displayed by groups has a rather simple explanation in a number of cases. More precisely, there exists a simple pooling hypothesis concerning member products that is at least *sufficient* to explain a rather wide range of group-individual results on decision-making, problem-solving, and learning tasks. However, the model developed by Taylor and by Lorge and Solomon does not explain *all* group performance. It has frequently *overpredicted* group performance, and this deviation remains to be explained in many cases. Furthermore, many different kinds of groups have not been studied in this individual-into-group manner, and hence their performance cannot be considered in light of this or other social combination hypotheses. The task and other circumstances frequently do not permit either empirical or mathematical construction of concocted groups.

We observed earlier that there has been an unfortunate tendency to regard the Taylor-Lorge-Solomon model as a "correction," as though real group products somehow contained an artifact, rather than as a theory about product-producing interpersonal processes. Like all theories, it stands until a more accurate, or more parsimonious, construction becomes available for the domain of phenomena to which it is applicable. Part of the artifact connotation may be due to the fact that some of the assumptions— for example, *independent* production of member responses—seem implausible in view of the usual observation that group members are typically far from passive. Even *ad hoc* laboratory groups working at an unexciting puzzle are ordinarily quite lively. Another reason for the artifact connotation may be due to the widespread feeling, traceable to earlier researchers, that groups should yield emergent solutions—solutions that are more than the "sum" or simple combination of their parts.

If a group does not operate at the level of its best member—the intellectual-hierarchy assumption of the Lorge-Solomon model—what social combination processes can be advanced to account for the final product, or even as another baseline against which group performance is to be judged in further research? Do some tasks foster or permit some decision or social combination schemes but not others? Moreover, some groups may have adopted a formal voting policy that contains implications for how the member contributions are to be combined.

In the following sections we shall continue to orient our discussion of the performance of interacting groups around the individual-group comparison. At the same time, however, we shall focus on the social combination schemes that have been advanced as models of the interaction processes responsible for the group output. Some of these schemes are intended as baselines, and some as actual descriptions of the group relationship between interaction and product.

Social Combination Processes: Problem Solving

Steiner (1966) has proposed several social combination schemes for judging *potential* group productivity, and we will follow his presentation closely. Optimal group performance is rarely attained, as we observed above; for potential productivity is reduced by losses due to faulty social process, especially motivation losses and interpersonal-coordination losses. Steiner (1966, pp. 273-274) has pointed out:

> The nature of the task determines whether a particular kind of resource (knowledge, ability, skill, or tool) is relevant, how much of each kind of resource is needed for optimal performance, and how the various relevant resources must be combined and utilized in order to produce the best possible outcome. . . . Unlike task demands and resources, process cannot be measured or evaluated before work begins. Process consists of the actual steps taken by an individual or a group when confronted with a task. It includes all those intrapersonal or interpersonal actions by which people transform their resources into a product, and all those nonproductive actions that are prompted by frustration, competing motivations, or inadequate understanding.

An *additive model* is one in which the task requires that all group members do exactly the same thing. The group response is the total of the members efforts. A rope pull is such a task, and assuming no faulty coordination or other losses, a team of four should pull twice as much as a group of two, or four times as much as an individual alone. It is perhaps no surprise to learn that the actual work performed by such groups is less than potential productivity. Dashiell (1935) has described a study by Ringlemann, who found that the mean pull exerted by two-, three-, and eight-person groups was 118, 160, and 248 kilograms, respectively, whereas perfect coordination and motivation would have yielded 126, 189, and 504 kilograms. It is interesting to note that Taylor and Faust (1952), studying groups faced with the more intellective but essentially summative task of Twenty Questions, likewise failed to find an improvement in speed proportional to the number of persons working on the task.

The *disjunctive model* proposed by Steiner has already been well exemplified by the Taylor-Lorge-Solomon hypothesis discussed earlier. The productivity of a group working at a common task is given by the productivity of its best member. The *conjunctive model* is very similar, and embodies the idea that group productivity is determined by the *least* competent member in the group where all members are required to do the same thing. One attractive feature of the conjunctive-disjunctive continuum is the possibility of *describing* the functioning of a nonoptimally performing group by finding whether or not the group can be characterized as performing at the level of its second, third, . . ., most competent member. Steiner and Rajaratnam (1961) took exactly this tack when they reanalyzed some of the results of an experiment by McCurdy and Lambert (1952). Steiner and Rajaratnam describe the experiment as follows (p. 145):

> Eleven individuals and thirteen three-person groups worked on a modified version of the Yerkes multiple-choice apparatus. Six two-position switches were wired so that a light appeared when the total pattern of switch positions corresponded to that on a master control panel. Individuals who worked alone were responsible for all six switches, whereas in the three-person groups each subject was responsible for two switches. Performance was measured by the number of correct switch patterns achieved during a period of 900 seconds. The mean performance of individuals who worked alone was found to be significantly superior to the mean performance of groups . . . .

McCurdy and Lambert had explained their rather unusual result of direct group inferiority by hypothesizing that at least one member of each group was a poor performer through inattention to instructions or the like. Steiner and Rajaratnam, however, substituted precise predictions for such plausible intuitions by setting up three hypotheses: (a) a group performed at the level of its most competent member, (b) its second most competent member, or (c) its third most competent member. Using the distribution of individual task abilities as an estimate of the population distribution and the manner in which percentiles might be expected to be distributed around population values, they tested their three hypotheses against actual group performance. They found that the first hypothesis, but not the second and third, could be confidently rejected. Apparently, groups were, at best, working at the level of their second most competent members.

The *compensatory model* describes the task-social process mentioned earlier in connection with the estimation of temperature, weights, etc. In cases where every member makes a judgment of the same stimulus, the mean of a set of judgments is generally a better estimate of the population mean than is a single person's judgment; we assume the population mean is equivalent to the "true" value. In other words, we are only saying that in most cases large samples provide better estimates of population parameters than do small samples. Such a situation obtains where decisions are liable to random error rather than constant error or bias, and these estimates are symmetrically distributed about the population mean. In essence, the compensatory model implies no more than is expressed by the formula for the standard error of the mean, which may be recalled from an elementary statistics course as

$$\sigma_{\bar{x}} = \sigma_x / \sqrt{N} ,$$

where $\sigma_{\bar{x}}$ is the standard error of the mean and σ_x is the standard deviation of a set of N measurements.

It is not difficult to imagine that a notion such as that exemplified by the compensatory model is learned informally by most persons in our culture. We may not only feel that it is democratic for the group to consider several opinions before making its response, but this procedure may also seem "intuitively" more likely to result in an accurate product. Of course, most people do not carry about the expression for the standard error of the mean in their heads.

Whereas the other Steiner models, described above, deal with the case in which the task requires all group members to do the same thing, the *complementary model* applies to those cases where the task can be *subdivided* and group members can divide their resources accordingly. When all members do the same thing, grouping can provide increased reliability through redundancy of effort or interpersonal stimulation. Despite these advantages, we have seen that groups are generally inefficient in such cases. Tasks permitting a division of labor, however, afford a number of additional opportunities for the utilization of member resources. At one extreme is the case where each member possesses a unique resource (information, skill, etc.), and at the other extreme there is overlap in resources among members. We observed earlier that the key problem is whether or not the group can organize itself, or be organized by an outside authority, in such a way that an optimal match can be arranged between task demands and resources. We also observed that group members assigned a logically and physically divisible task can work simultaneously on different parts of the problem by organizing themselves and allocating subtasks to members. Overlap of effort is thus avoided and troublesome parts can receive more than their share of attention, since early-finishing members can aid their slower companions.

From preceding sections it should be evident that there are strong social forces preventing groups from easily attaining such optimal organizations—

at least those with brief histories and tasks that are not easily divisible. How *do* informal groups organize themselves? Do groups attacking physically divisible problems achieve a closer approach to optimal task performance?

Recall that the Lorge-Solomon Model B was designed for tasks composed of several subelements. Model B was described earlier as the application of Model A at each step of a task comprised of several such parts. That is to say, at each step, one assumes that social interaction is neither helpful nor detrimental and that the group will solve that subproblem if it contains at least one member who solves it; in other words, "the truth wins" each time. Members are assumed to act independently, and each subproblem is solved independently of every other. The process is complete when all subproblems are solved. (Again, such notions seem implausible in practice, but the resulting baseline can be used to evaluate the kind of social process that might be involved in groups working on divisible tasks.) For example, imagine that there is a two-part problem to be solved and an individual can be right or wrong on either or both parts. A population of such persons would appear as the following (see Lorge and Solomon, 1955):

Population Type	Ability	Proportion in the Population
X_1	Solve both stages	P_1
X_2	Solve stage 1, not stage 2	P_2
X_3	Solve stage 2, not stage 1	P_3
X_4	Solve neither stage	P_4

An individual solves if and only if he is of type X_1, but if he fails to solve he might be an X_2, X_3, or X_4 type. A group has the capability of solving even if it contains no X_1 persons. The exact probability of a group solution depends on group size and the probability of the stages being solved. Consider groups of size four as an example: $(X_1, X_4, X_4, X_3), (X_2, X_2, X_3, X_4), (X_4, X_3, X_3, X_4)$. The first two groups solve, but not the third. The second group does not contain a solver, but is able to solve because the partial solutions can be put together through social interaction—if the necessary social organization or information exchange patterns can be developed. This latter matter is the interesting question for freely interacting groups.

A number of different tasks could be imagined within this framework other than those permitting the dichotomy between solution and nonsolution. However, by way of illustration, let us consider an experiment by Olson and Davis (1964) in which an easily divisible task was assigned both to individuals and to four-person groups. The task was completed when each of five separate and self-contained arithmetic problems had been answered. *Ad hoc* groups were instructed to interact freely and to organize themselves, if they wished, in any manner they found comfortable or helpful in attacking the problem. The proportion of solutions among the 25 groups significantly exceeded that among the 49 individual subjects (.64 versus .04, respectively) when the problem was considered as a whole, and groups were higher on every subproblem as well. The Lorge-Solomon Model A baseline was significantly *exceeded* by group performance (.15 versus .64, respectively), but the subproblem-pooling Model B significantly *overpredicted* group performance (.86 versus .64).

Olson and Davis concluded after close observation of group discussion that members tended to work as much toward agreement as toward solution. Groups generally tended to organize for work by allocating the subproblems, but most interaction was directed toward establishing an affable atmosphere.

Part of this group tendency may perhaps be due to the fact that members grow up in a democratic culture in which a kind of equalitarianism is valued, but there is also the logical dilemma of a group attempting to organize itself *prior to sustained interaction.* The interaction might reveal a more rational basis for subtask allocation than merely breaking up a divisible problem at random. That is to say, individual differences in *ability* were not evident prior to discussion, and perhaps not clearly discernible even after the short (20-minute) discussion period. At least, agreeable discussion and interaction organized along equalitarian lines has the virtue of a kind of "social survival value." A group that remains in existence long enough to discover members' talents could eventually organize for a more satisfactory use of resources—namely, an intellectual hierarchy that is correlated with member skills.

The idea of an equalitarian group structure arising "naturally" to mediate the input-output relationship was proposed formally by Restle and Davis (1962) and tested in part by Davis and Restle (1963). The problems used by Davis and Restle were not physically divisible in the manner we have been discussing, yet were apparently composed of stages, each of which had to be solved successively before the task was completed. Such tasks are in some ways similar to both the disjunctive-conjunctive and complementary processes outlined by Steiner.

Davis and Restle administered three eureka problems that required subjects to discover how a prisoner could manipulate a rope to escape from a tower, untangle a word twister containing self-defeating phrases, and solve a modified "water jar problem" in which containers had to be manipulated to obtain a particular final volume. Group performance significantly exceeded that of individuals working alone. However, performance in the four-person groups fell below predictions from a social combination model called the Hierarchical Model. The model's name served to emphasize the implicit assumption that the "truth wins" idea actually requires a group to form an intellectual hierarchy that gives preeminence to those subjects who

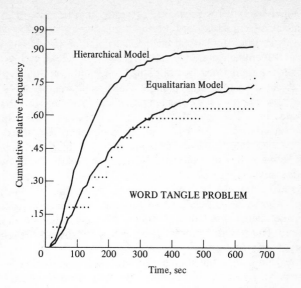

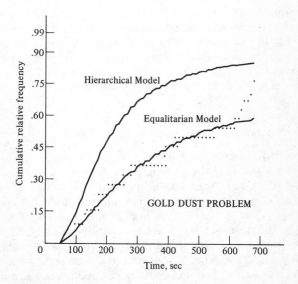

Fig. 3.4 The cumulative relative frequency of group solutions (closed points) and predictions from the Hierarchical and Equalitarian Models. (From Davis and Restle, 1963. Copyright 1963 by the American Psychological Association, and reproduced by permission.)

are on the right track. We have already suggested that this idea is implausible in the usual short-term laboratory group.

However, another model had been constructed on the social hypothesis that *all* group members shared equally the group's working time, whether they were on the right track or not. This "fair play" hypothesis about the emergent social structure was named the Equalitarian Model, and was intended to *describe* the social process rather than serve merely as a baseline to determine the efficiency of effort. In other words, the Equalitarian Model was an attempt to account for the group performance decrement detected as a baseline deviation in a number of similar experiments. The agreement between the two models and real group data (from two of the problems) is shown in Fig. 3.4.

Davis and Restle also collected some observational data concerning the interaction patterns that developed during work, and administered post-session questionnaires that asked members to indicate their feelings about one another. These data generally agreed with the hypothesis of an equalitarian group structure.

We have found that the members of freely interacting *ad hoc* groups rarely arrange an optimal interpersonal structure to process efficiently the information demanded by the problem. Group performance is rarely at the level of its best member, and thus most often drops below the baseline describing optimal performance. Such a conclusion seems to hold even when the task and circumstances permit a division of labor; the group rarely organizes itself in such a way as to exploit the advantages from pooling partial solutions. At least one hypothesis about the interpersonal combination of member contributions (equalitarianism) permits a theoretical description of group problem solving, but the source of the social restraint is often not clear.

Social Combination Processes: Learning

What sort of social mechanism is likely to explain the group product when the task requires primarily that information be stored and retrieved at some point? Although there is reason to believe that "learning groups" tend to perform roughly in accord with the Lorge-Solomon Model A baseline (see Hoppe, 1962), there is not a great deal of evidence about how group members go about storing and retrieving information when the task demands it. (Hoppe's subjects, it might be recalled, were not permitted to divide the task of learning a list of nonsense words among themselves.)

Whereas the together and apart studies, discussed earlier in connection with social facilitation and inhibition, concentrated heavily on learning tasks, the same emphasis has not been applied in studies of groups of *interacting* members. One important exception has been the work of Laughlin and his associates (Laughlin, 1965; Laughlin and Doherty, 1967; Laughlin and McGlynn, in press; Laughlin, McGlynn, Anderson, and

Jacobson, 1968) in which a concept attainment task was presented to subjects working alone and to other subjects working together as a cooperative group. The basic idea in a concept attainment task is that, over a sequence of trials or over time, the subject learns that some stimulus events belong together and thus are instances of the concept, whereas other stimulus events are not instances of it. In essence, stimulus objects are grouped or classified in such a way that all members of a class have something in common, although they may also possess a wide variety of other features that are not held in common. The task used by Laughlin was as follows (Laughlin, McGlynn, Anderson, and Jacobson, 1968, p. 410):

> . . . [the subject] faces an array of cards varying on a number of attributes (shape, color, etc.) with two or more values of each attribute (triangle or square, red or green, etc.). The experimenter arbitrarily designates a combination of two or more values (e.g., red triangle) as a concept, and indicates an initial card that satisfies this concept. The problem solver must then determine what combination has been designated by selecting a card, learning whether or not the card exemplifies the concept, making a hypothesis, feedback on the hypothesis, and repeating the cycle until he reasons to the solution. The sequence of card choices and hypotheses may be analyzed to determine the strategy or problem-solving process used.

As we have come to expect, Laughlin has found that cooperative pairs typically achieve the concept in fewer card choices than do individuals, and at the same time come up with fewer untenable hypotheses along the way. What is perhaps more interesting is that groups tend to favor one kind of strategy (focusing) in attaining the concept, while individuals favor another (scanning): "In focusing S [the subject] tests the relevance of all the possible hypotheses involved in a particular attribute or attributes . . . . In scanning he tests specific hypotheses . . ." (Laughlin, 1965, p. 323). Focusing is a more successful strategy, for the memory requirements of scanning put rather heavy demands on the person doing it.

Two-person groups not only show a preference for the more efficient strategy in attaining the concept, they also perform at a level closely in accord with predictions from concocted groups constructed according to the assumptions of the Taylor-Lorge-Solomon model. In other words, these groups do no better than their best member. While discussion appears to be more important to group performance than memory aids (e.g., pencil and paper), and cooperative pairs give better results than competitive pairs, there appears to be little direct evidence as to *how* pairs achieve their product. Laughlin *et al.* (1968) have suggested that there are "facilitative processes" at work in the groups which are absent in the individuals. It does seem that the better performer of the pair dominates in determining the product; that is, the pair is a two-person hierarchy. However, no evidence exists that there is a better *type* of *individual* corresponding to each type of problem who is consistently dominant. Group performance at the level of the better member might therefore be due to the self-confirming nature of a correct strategy, for it is highly visible in such a task. Thus if the better contribution is always dominant, and one ignores the notion of a stable "concept ability," then it is not necessary to evoke any other facilitative process beyond the members and their exchange of information during discussion.

Again, very little is known about the small group as an information acquisition and storage mechanism. Laughlin and his associates have provided one of the few lines of precise experimental investigation of group performance with tasks emphasizing learning.

Like problem solving, the storage of information in a group of persons should be affected by the way the group resolves its division-of-labor obstacles. How do groups organize themselves to parcel out subtasks when that is possible? At this point we shall only describe briefly a logical attack on the question of how information (such as a set of items) can be assigned to a group of r individuals in such a way that each item has the maximum probability of being recalled. If any individual in a group recalls the information, then we shall assume that the information is available to the group.

Zajonc and Smoke (1959) attacked just this optimization problem and arrived at some surprising results. Since memory is imperfect in a single member, more than one person should have some of the same information. However, the assignment of a large quantity of information to a single member results in poorer recall than if each member has fewer items to store and retrieve. Zajonc and Smoke assumed that the probability of recalling each item is constant for all items and all members. Consequently, each item should be assigned to an equal number of group members and the same number of items should be assigned to all members. With these simplifying assumptions, they found (Zajonc, 1966, p. 107) that the most efficient division of labor occurs when

> ... each individual is assigned a number of items which will result in his remembering only 84 percent of them.... The solution tells us namely that we should overload our group members by 16 percent, regardless of how many of them make up the group, and regardless of how much total work there is—a curious result that we would not suspect intuitively. Of course, the number of people to which each item is assigned ... will vary with the size of the group and the size of the group task.

Even though persons differ in recall ability, the overload per person should be 16 percent. That the optimal overload per person is independent of so many variables is both surprising and provocative, but has yet to be checked thoroughly against real groups whose primary task is the collective storage and recall of information.

TABLE 3.1

A Description of Several Decision Schemes Frequently
Used in Formal Voting or Implied in Informal Decisions

Title	Decision Scheme Description
Dictatorship	The group response is completely determined by the response of one particular individual, who may be the group leader, an expert, or an adviser.
Oligarchy	The group response of r individuals is completely determined by the *joint response* of a *particular subset or subgroup* of the larger group, the subgroup always being smaller than the parent group.
Unanimity	The group response is A if and only if *all* members respond A; otherwise, alternative B is the response.
Fixed	The group response is A if and only if some *exact number* of members respond A. The size of this subgroup is fixed at some number equal to or less than the size of the parent group.
Quorum	The group response is A if and only if *at least* some number of the members respond A; otherwise, alternative B is the response. This quorum must be equal to or smaller than the parent group.
Minimal Quorum	The group response is A if and only if *at least one* (there may be more) *member's* response is A, and is alternative B otherwise.
Independent	The group response is independent of member responses and is determined by an external criterion or authority. The probability of this external criterion imposing alternative A is fixed at some constant value that is unchanged by anything the group does.

Note. This table is developed from a similar list by Smoke and Zajonc (1962).

Social Combination Processes: Decision Making

To conceptualize group interaction as a social combination scheme seems perhaps even more natural when one is discussing decision tasks than either of the other two types of tasks we have been considering. For one thing, there is frequently a *formal* decision rule or voting mechanism which permits the group to arrive at one or a few alternatives out of several confronting it. It is well known that many established groups resolve conflicts or translate individual preferences into a group product by tallying the distribution of preferences among group members during or after discussion of the possibilities. It is perhaps less obvious that, even in the absence of overt vote tallying, discussion of the task nevertheless indicates

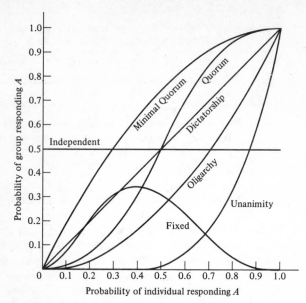

Fig 3.5   Various decision schemes for groups of five. The Oligarchy, Fixed Subgroup, and Quorum size has been set at two. The probability of an independent external criterion requiring an *A* decision has been set at .5. (Reproduced by permission from Smoke and Zajonc, 1962.)

publicly the members' preferences. The final group decision is thus some function of the ultimate preference distribution and the implicit decision scheme.

The problem confronting the student of group decision behavior is virtually the same as that encountered with group problem solving. What social decision scheme can translate the individual preference distribution into a group decision? What are the effects of social interaction that must be incorporated in a theoretical model of that decision scheme? First, we might consider the individual preference distribution across a set of alternatives, and then ask: To what group decision (if one and only one must be chosen) do various schemes or mechanisms lead? One such set of decision schemes is listed in Table 3.1. This table deals with the simplest case, in which there are only two alternatives, *A* and *B*. One of these alternatives, for convenience, may even be labeled correct or superior, and the other incorrect or inferior. In other words, supposing there is some probability of an individual choosing *A*, we seek the probability that a group will yield decision *A* under the various decision schemes. (This discussion draws heavily upon the work of Smoke and Zajonc, 1962.)

Figure 3.5 shows, for groups of size five under various decision schemes, the probability that a group will respond with *A* as a function of the probability that an individual preference is A. The figure suggests several conclusions. If we imagine alternative A to be the "correct" one, then the democratic idea that decisions should somehow be based on a quorum scheme of some sort may have more to recommend it than simple intuition or social virtue. But this observation holds mainly where there is already a high preference for the correct alternative in the population from which the group is drawn. The appeal of a dictatorship, on the other hand, is most evident when the reverse is true. The liabilities of oligarchies and of the unanimity requirement are self-evident from Fig. 3.5. (It is worth noting that the Minimal Quorum scheme of Fig. 3.5 is formally identical to Lorge and Solomon's Model A.)

The preceding discussion could be extended to tasks allowing more than the two decision alternatives we have been considering. However, the convenient reduction of many-alternative dilemmas into a dichotomy (right-wrong, good-bad, yes-no) seems to occur regularly both in the psychological laboratory and in real life.

Once several potential task responses have been constructed by members, the selection of one or more of these for the final group product might entail substantial conflict and require the use of compromise after lengthy discussion. Two especially interesting cases may be distinguished in group decision making:

a) The group has a formal decision scheme dictated by custom or authority, but the scheme is in existence prior to the group's confrontation with the goal.

b) The group does not possess a formal decision-making or conflict-resolving scheme, and must develop such a scheme as well as the decision itself.

It is quite a common observation that groups, both *ad hoc* groups and those with traditions, can and do make quite complex decisions without a formal vote or any decisive overt action.

The League of Women Voters is an excellent example of this latter case. A League chapter does not actually vote, but "consensuses" during meetings. That is to say, discussion precedes any decision on the stand to be taken on some issue before the group; but the decision is a consequence of a subtle social process that ends up with the presiding officer announcing that such and such a course of action is the consensus of the group. Discussion continues in this way until there is no objection to the summary statement (decision) regarding the group's course of action. It is not clear whether or not we should regard this as a true unanimity scheme.

In most informal discussions, of course, the expression of opinion (especially on the part of high-status members) may effectively constitute a kind of vote. The important empirical challenge is finding the *de facto* interpersonal combination-decision scheme that produces the group response.

Little experimental research exists concerning the social dynamics of groups working on formal decision schemes assigned by custom or authority. Informal *ad hoc* decision-making groups, on the other hand, have been studied for a long time. In either case, there are important reasons for comparing the decision making of individuals and groups. A number of governmental, industrial, military, and other institutional groups exist within their parent organizations mainly in order to arrive at judicious decisions for which the consequences seem, intuitively, too important to be left to a single individual. As may be inferred from the preceding sections, this intuition is sometimes well founded, but it always reflects a complex question.

Risk taking. There are many kinds of decision-making groups that we might consider if space permitted. We will further illustrate the topic by focusing on a particular area of individual-group decision making: risk taking. We have paid little attention until now to the consequences of decisions, in terms of either anticipated or actual feedback. This is an important aspect of group decisions.

Individual decisions may be studied in several ways, but the idea that a person may lose as well as gain something in the process has often been a dominant theme. The risks or uncertainties surrounding the execution of decisions constitute an important class of variables. In fact, decision situations entailing risks arise frequently in the lives of most of us. Furthermore, groups seem to be an especially attractive setting for important decisions which involve a high degree of uncertainty.

One frequently has some crude personal estimate of the desirability of the payoff attached to the various outcomes of decisions, but less commonly a knowledge of the "actual" probability of occurrence of the various outcomes. When the subject must construct a personal or subjective probability from past experience or intuition, his preferences are said to be *decisions under uncertainty.* If the odds are "given," as in horse racing and dice games, it is common practice to speak of *decisions under risk.* "Given probabilities," however, are often illusory, and in most applications the formal status of these objective probabilities is unclear. The payoffs (what may be gained or lost) are sometimes scaled according to their attractiveness or subjective value to the subject. However, for many interesting decision situations this empirical scaling of outcomes is unfortunately not possible, and the investigator is denied the knowledge of the relative subjective utility of the various outcomes. In any event, the usual procedure in studying individual decisions is to require that the subject make a choice among two or more outcomes, either as a one-shot affair or as part of a sequence of such decisions. A number of situational and personal variables have been related to such decisions, as well as the obvious task variables such as amounts of payoffs, patterns of outcomes, probabilities of outcomes.

At this point we might digress to the extent of mentioning that *theoretical* attempts to understand individual decision making have often made use of probability theory. In addition, *experimental* attempts to study decisions under risk or uncertainty have often used the language of games of chance, or have even used a standard gambling game (or some adaptation of one) as the experimental task. Many existing games of chance do resemble, at least in outline, a number of real-life decision situations and afford substantial experimental control over task and surrounding conditions. In many such gambling tasks it is possible to calculate the average winnings of a player supposing he were to play indefinitely. This average, also called an *expected value,* is calculated by weighting the payoff of the outcome by its probability and summing over all possible outcomes. Another constant feature (or *parameter*) of such well-defined processes, and one which is also studied in connection with subjects' gaming preferences, is the *variance.* The expected value of two decision processes might be identical, but one of them might yield fairly uniform probabilities and payoffs over the outcomes, while the other process might possess widely differing probabilities and payoffs; thus the latter would have a larger variance.

A number of other parameters of the task-dependent processes also exist, but it appears that no single parameter can be said to determine decision behavior for *all* situations involving human choices. Sometimes expected value, or variance, or both serve to yield good accounts of decisions—if some estimate of outcome probability and payoff is known to the investigator. But very often the necessary information about the process the decision maker actually faces is not available to the researcher, and thus it is difficult to reconstruct the situation as it appears to the subject. It is worth emphasizing that there is no evidence that subjects in fact *compute* parameter values in the way their experimenters sometimes do. There is even evidence that subjects *trained* in the computation and use of expected value are poor users of this information (Lichtenstein, Slovic, and Zinc, 1968). Nevertheless, subjects may use a subjective estimate or response strategy in some decision situations that is closely related to one or more of the formal task parameters we have discussed. Also, expected value may serve as a kind of baseline for individual (or group) decisions (we discussed the baseline function earlier in connection with group learning and problem solving).

We may distinguish two extremes among the current approaches to the study of group risk taking:

a)   One approach tends to present subjects (individuals and groups) with a decision task that has some apparent relevance to real-life situations, but allows the researcher rather limited control of task qualities.

b)   At the other extreme, the decision task confronting subjects does not necessarily have a social situation as a direct referent; rather it is intended to include the essential risk-taking variables and parameters in a way that permits close experimental control.

The former sacrifices some precision to achieve some realism, while the latter sacrifices some realism to attain some precision. We shall consider each in turn, and at the same time pursue our concern with possible social decision-combination schemes.

Choice dilemmas and the risky shift. One important line of decision research has assessed the inclination of a subject to take a risk by presenting him with a *miniature social situation,* called a choice dilemma, in which a choice must be made between two courses of action (Marquis, 1962; Kogan and Wallach, 1967); each of the alternatives has a "good" outcome and a "bad" outcome. Usually several choice dilemmas are presented in questionnaire form, and the respondent is asked to advise a person who is faced with each of the dilemmas. For one course of action the positive outcome is supposed to be moderately desirable and it is fairly likely to occur. For the other alternative the positive outcome is thought to be *very* attractive, but not very probable. The subject is required to indicate, for each dilemma, the *minimum odds* (lowest probability) that he would accept and still advise the imaginary central figure to choose the more attractive, but less likely, alternative. The lower the acceptable odds, the more willing the subject is to take a risk. Several items (taken from Kogan and Wallach, 1967) of the choice-dilemma type are presented below:

Mr. D is the captain of College X's football team. College X is playing its traditional rival, College Y, in the final game of the season. The game is in its final seconds, and Mr. D's team, College X, is behind in the score. College X has time to run one more play. Mr. D, captain, must decide whether it would be best to settle for a tie score with a play which would be almost certain to work or, on the other hand, should he try a more complicated and risky play which would bring victory if it succeeded, but defeat if not.

Imagine that you are advising Mr. D. Listed below are several probabilities or odds that the risky play will work.

Please check the *lowest* probability that you would consider acceptable for the risky play to be attempted.

_____ Place a check here if you think Mr. D should *not* attempt the risky play no matter what the probabilities.

_____ The chances are 9 in 10 that the risky play will work.

_____ The chances are 7 in 10 that the risky play will work.

_____ The chances are 5 in 10 that the risky play will work.

_____ The chances are 3 in 10 that the risky play will work.

_____ The chances are 1 in 10 that the risky play will work.

Mr. G, a competent chess player, is participating in a national chess tournament. In an early match he draws the top-favored player in the tournament as his opponent. Mr. G has been given a relatively low ranking in view of his performance in previous tournaments. During the course of his play with the top-favored man, Mr. G notes the possibility of a deceptive though risky maneuver which might bring him a quick victory. At the same time, if the attempted maneuver should fail, Mr. G would be left in an exposed position and defeat would almost certainly follow.

Imagine that you are advising Mr. G. Listed below are several probabilities or odds that Mr. G's deceptive play would succeed. . . .

Mr. M is contemplating a marriage to Miss T, a girl whom he has known for a little more than a year. Recently, however, a number of arguments have occurred between them, suggesting some sharp differences of opinion in the way each views certain matters. Indeed, they decide to seek professional advice from a marriage counselor as to whether it would be wise for them to marry. On the basis of these meetings with a marriage counselor, they realize that a happy marriage, while possible, would not be assured.

Imagine that you are advising Mr. M and Miss T. Listed below are several probabilities or odds that their marriage would prove to be a happy and successful one. . . .

Mr. B, a married man with two children, has a steady job that pays him about $6000 per year. He can easily afford the necessities of life, but few of the luxuries. Mr. B's father, who died recently, carried a $4000 life insurance policy. Mr. B would like to invest this money in stocks. He is well aware of the secure "blue chip" stocks and bonds that would pay approximately 6% on his investment. On the other hand, Mr. B has heard that the stocks of a relatively unknown Company X might double their present value if a new product currently in production is favorably received by the buying public. On the other hand, if the product is unfavorably received, the stocks would decline in value.

Imagine that you are advising Mr. B. Listed below are several probabilities or odds that Company X stocks will double their value. . . .

The matter of primary interest here is the comparison of private individual decisions with (a) the collective decision given by groups and (b) the private decisions of group members following group discussion. The first experiments revealed the very interesting result that when *individuals* who had previously made their private decisions engaged in *group* discussion, the group decisions were riskier (Marquis, 1962; Wallach, Kogan, and Bem, 1962). This change toward greater risk is evident not only in the unanimous or majority decision of the group, but also in private post-discussion individual preferences (see Kogan and Wallach, 1967). Like most other experimental groups we have considered, these decision groups were given no rules or schemes for resolving conflicts, or suggestions as to how they should discuss the choice. The shift toward risky decisions, or the "risky shift" as it has sometimes been called, has obvious practical as well as theoretical implications. Many different groups in our culture make important decisions that profoundly affect a large number of people. Thus it is important to identify any built-in mechanism that might tend to bias the direction of collective decision. What sort of internal mechanism might be operating to transform individual inputs into a group product inclined toward risk? Does group discussion change the personal decisions of the members? Or does the social combination process effected through interaction weight risky decisions more heavily? Or do both of these things occur?

A number of explanations for the risky shift have been proposed, but the most popular may be grouped into three general classes:

a)   Group members favoring high risk are more influential than low risk takers. Discussion following the initial expression of preference affords high risk advocates the opportunity to influence low risk takers more than they themselves are influenced in turn.

b)   The making of a *group* decision allows the group members to "diffuse responsibility" for that decision, so that any cost or imagined loss could be shared by all. Sharing risk in this way permits groups to decide in favor of riskier alternatives.

c)   Group discussion permits the sharing of information about other persons' risk-taking proclivities as well as further information about the task itself. When a member finds that he is not far ahead of the central tendency (as revealed by his own group's norm), but near or below it, he tends to revise his estimate in favor of being more extreme than when he filled out the questionnaire the first time. In this latter case, we assume that the content of the item (choice dilemma) engages a social value. For example, the spirit of "nothing ventured, nothing gained" is an apt guide to the football captain in the situation described on page 62; one "should" take a risk here. When group discussion reveals that one is not commendably ahead of others, then a revision toward greater risk is desirable.

Hypothesis (a) (that high-risk subjects are persuasive) has been favored by some researchers (e.g., Collins and Guetzkow, 1964), but others (e.g., Kogan and Wallach, 1967) reject it as unconvincing. However, slight positive correlations between riskiness and persuasiveness have sometimes been encountered (Flanders and Thistlethwaite, 1967; Wallach, Kogan and Burt, 1968; Wallach, Kogan, and Bem, 1962). Kogan and Wallach's explanation is that groups already turning to risk will as a matter of course contain members who perceive, after the fact, that riskier members were influential; this is a matter of determining which is cause and which is effect. Not only have Kogan and Wallach on one occasion found a slight negative correlation between risk and influence, but they have designed an experiment to test the influence hypothesis in a direct way (Wallach, Kogan, and Burt, 1968).

Wallach *et al.,* in this latter experiment, assessed the degree of risk taking by pretesting subjects with the usual choice-dilemma questionnaire several months prior to the experiment. They also required subjects to respond to a set of similar items that were "risk neutral," using the customary sequence (individual decisions, then group discussion with decision) of earlier work. The assignment of subjects to the five-person groups was such that risk-taking tendencies were evenly distributed within the group. Group members also rated each other on persuasiveness and other interpersonal qualities. The main finding was that risk taking and persuasiveness following discussion and group decision on the "risk neutral" items were not significantly related for male groups, and were marginally related for females. In general, the findings were against the notion that advocating risky decisions imparts persuasiveness to the advocate.

The importance of the content of the items in the above experiment holds some interesting implications for the other two hypotheses—responsibility diffusion and information about peer norms. First of all, the diffusion-of-responsibility hypothesis is difficult to evaluate directly, for the choice-dilemma task does not provoke the kind of overt behavior that permits a clear differentiation between the subject who is diffusing and the one who is not thus sharing his perceived risk. Consequently the research strategy has been to discredit, at least in part, the diffusion hypothesis by showing that diffusion is not necessary, although it might turn out to be sufficient to produce the risky shift.

The most nearly direct evidence for the diffusion-of-responsibility hypothesis comes from a study by Wallach, Kogan, and Bem (1964) on intellective problem solving. The experiment is described as follows (Kogan and Wallach, 1967, p. 261):

> . . . some subjects were made to feel responsible for the wins and losses of the other group members as well as for their own. Furthermore, responsibility for others was created under two kinds of circumstances for different subjects; some of them had to decide on their preferred risk-taking levels individually, but others made their decisions through group discussion to consensus. While the former condition yielded conservative shifts, the latter resulted in strong shifts toward greater risk taking. Thus, responsibility for others coupled with group discussion and its opportunity for sharing of this responsibility not only overcomes the conservatism that results when such responsibility is created without the opportunity for discussion but also adds a considerable push toward taking more risk. . . . The second kind of evidence in support of the responsibility-diffusion concept pertains to the contrast . . . between two kinds of group conditions. In one, group decisions were made, but with the knowledge that any one member might be responsible for the wins and losses of all group members. While discussion produced a risky shift in both conditions, the risky shift was larger when responsibility was felt for others as well as for oneself. Added responsibility under circumstances where it can be shared by group discussion thus seems to enhance risk taking.

In arguing against the diffusion hypothesis, Marquis (1968) has pointed out that, when a leader from near the middle of the risk-taking distribution was made solely responsible for the decision, that leader shifted to greater risk on the second occasion along with his advisers, who had no direct responsibility (Marquis, 1962).

A number of other studies also cast doubt on the hypothesis that diffusion of responsibility is the sole mechanism underlying the risky shift (e.g., Flanders and Thistlethwaite, 1967), but we shall turn at this point to the third hypothesis—that the choice dilemma engages a cultural value concerning risk, and group discussion permits the subject to make a more accurate appraisal as to where he stands with regard to the population norm. Since Brown (1965) first proposed this hypothesis in a general way, a number of investigators have used it for interpreting experimental results (e.g., Teger and Pruitt, 1967) or have devised direct experimental tests of the notion (e.g., Stoner, 1967).

Before examining the evidence for the value-norm hypothesis, we shall consider two important matters that are ignored in the influence and diffusion hypotheses, but are conveniently included in the value-norm idea: (a) the *specific task* and its content, and (b) the *individual preference distribution* existing *prior* to group discussion. Both the influence and diffusion explanations deal with personal or interpersonal features of the social setting, yet each of the twelve choice dilemmas describes a different situation, and subjects respond differently to them. Do all of these items, or other items of the same general form, yield the same results with both individuals and groups? The answer to this question is that they do not.

One of the original twelve items was observed to yield frequently a *cautious shift*. That is, in various studies the group decision was more cautious than the prediscussion individual decision on an item (the case of Mr. M contemplating marriage, quoted earlier). More important, Nordhøy (1962) wrote some choice-dilemma items that were similar in form to the original set, but on which the group decision was generally more *cautious* than the prior individual decisions. Finally, Stoner (1967) conducted a study, within the now familiar paradigm, in which two kinds of choice-dilemma items were used. For the set on which individual subjects considered themselves relatively risky and which were judged to reflect widely held values as to the desirability of risky behavior, the group decisions were indeed riskier than the individual decisions. For the second set of items, the opposite conditions held and the result was a cautious shift for groups.

It thus appears that *both* a cautious and a risky shift must be considered for some tasks. If the item content is such that the subject population generally believes risk (or caution) to be valuable, then the individual subject tends to respond so that he is at least as risky (or cautious) as others. Group discussion then reveals that some subjects are not up to the group norm, and as a result the subject changes his decision to greater risk (or caution), thereby altering the average risk-taking level. Thus both group decisions and post-discussion private decisions would reflect the change, and of course shifts have been observed in both formats (see Kogan and Wallach, 1967).

In summary, it appears that the group shift in choice-dilemma decisions has the effect of exacerbating the tendencies reflected in the prior individual preference distribution, and that the original decisions of individuals are dependent on how individuals perceive the content of the dilemma. The norm-value explanation of group shift phenomena, due primarily to Brown (1965) and Marquis (1962, 1968), describes the kind of social combination process that may be at work in the interaction which yields the group decision. However, the nature of the choice-dilemma task hinders the construction of a theoretical model for predicting the direction and degree of the group shift with the norm-value hypothesis. As we mentioned earlier, the dilemmas are intriguing to subjects and have the attractive feature of apparent realism. However, the structure of the basic task is not clear; the relative attractiveness of the imagined payoff to subjects is difficult to assess, and the relationship between positive and negative outcomes both within and between alternatives is often fuzzy. We will turn next to decision tasks that permit somewhat closer control over task structure, although they lack the engaging realism of the dilemma items.

Structured choice tasks and group decisions. Some decision tasks permit the subject to develop his own estimate of the probabilities that certain outcomes will arise, to learn the kind of benefits (payoff values) associated with outcomes, and actually to experience feedback directly after decision. These features imply repeated task experience in that a number of decisions are required over a sequence of trials. Davis, Hoppe, and Hornseth (1968) used such a repeated-decisions task in an experiment designed, in part, to explore the generality of the group-shift phenomenon, and also to explore one idea about what the social combination process or group decision scheme might be in such a case.

Davis *et al.* employed a task where the subject (individual or four-person group) decided either to stay with a *known* outcome (win or lose one unit of the stake) that occurred first on each of several trials, or take a risk by deciding to accept an *unknown* outcome (win or lose up to 11 units) that occurred as the second event on each trial. Groups were free to choose in any way they wished following discussion. The expected value of both known and unknown outcomes was actually zero, and each particular outcome was equally likely. The results indicated that a plurality decision scheme (whereby the group accepted the response strategy preferred by the largest number of members) was a fair description of the social combination process within groups; but the evidence was not decisive. The direct comparison of individuals and groups, however, gave no evidence of the group shift. Other studies with such tasks (e.g., Lonergan and McClintock, 1961) had also failed to encounter the risky or cautious shift observed regularly with choice-dilemma questionnaires.

Is the absence of a detectable group shift in the studies by Davis *et al.* and Lonergan and McClintock due to the fact that tasks differ from dilemmas questionnaires in some way, or to procedural differences? (In the above two studies, individuals and groups were *independent* in that group members had no previous decision experience with the task.) The answer apparently lies once more in task features, for other structured decision tasks have resulted in group shifts.

Zajonc, Wolosin, Wolosin, and Sherman (1968a, 1968b) also designed an experiment to test the generality of the group shift and to ascertain the kind of decision scheme that might give a sufficient account of the social combination process yielding the group decision. Their task was in many ways similar to that used by Davis *et al.* However, the payoffs involved small amounts of money rather than points, and the decision alternatives were simpler and perhaps clearer.

Zajonc *et al.* (1968a) have observed that the evidence from the dilemma studies implying individual *member preference changes* was actually indecisive. Could it be that individual changes in risk taking were not a *cause* of the group shift, but a consequence of the group decision reached by discussion? Thus the important shift mechanism might be adherence to a group decision scheme rather than interpersonal influence, responsibility diffusion, or social values. Zajonc *et al.* required subjects to select one of two lights prior to each of several trials. One of the lights appeared at random on 60 percent of the trials, and the other on 40 percent. If the subject preselected the less frequent light, he received one and a half cents; if he selected the more frequent, he gained one cent. Subjects received nothing for incorrect selections. All subjects made individual decisions for 180 trials; for a second identical set of 180 trials, half of the subjects continued as before, but the other half were assigned to three-person groups. Unanimous group decisions were required during the discussion period immediately preceding the light, and groups were informed that *each person* would be paid off at the same rate as before when the *group* was correct. Significantly *fewer* risks (selecting the less frequent but more rewarding light) were taken by groups than by individuals during the second set of trials. Groups were also less risky on the second set of trials than their members had been when working alone on the first set.

The cautious shift was large. The task contained no social content and the responsibility for winning and losing (payoff plan) was the same for groups as for individuals. Thus some mechanism associated with grouping or the task structure, or both, must be responsible. Thinking along these lines, Zajonc *et al.* compared the group data with predictions from various decision schemes that we discussed earlier. Simple majority, unanimity, average, and a dictatorship by several different "kinds" of members (most conservative, risky, moderate, and successful) were all inadequate in predicting group results. Zajonc *et al.* concluded finally that the group discussion may have produced a revision in the utilities or perceived value of the payoffs, rather than an increase or decrease in risk taking *per se*. The simple fact that their choices were shown to be right or wrong in public may have influenced the subjects to choose the more frequently occurring alternative more often than the less frequently occurring one. By doing so they achieved a higher total "return."

Such a revision of utilities implies a genuine change in individual members' preferences. However, a second study by the same authors (Zajonc, Wolosin, Wolosin, and Sherman, 1968b) led to the conclusion that an implicit decision scheme might after all be involved in group interaction leading to the final decision. The second study replicated and extended the earlier findings, and led to a simple theoretical model of both individual and group risk taking in such situations. The *individual model* assumes that the objective probabilities of the lights (.60 and .40) account for some subjects' preferences, while others' are uncertain (not stable). The resolution of these latter subjects' indecision is dependent on the ratio of the payoffs between the two lights. The *group decision model* assumes that members do not change their preferences during interaction and that the important determinant is the probability that a group contains members having a particular preference. Some groups are initially unanimous, of course, but others are not. Divided groups are unstable, and this instability requires the additional assumption that resolution proceeds by taking into account the total joint payoff expected by the majority and minority members. We lack the space here to describe the two models in greater detail, but their predictions agree well with data on both group and individual decisions.

As Zajonc *et al.* point out, their explanation of group shifts places more emphasis than do other explanations on the actual *expected outcomes of decisions.* Other investigators seem now to be favoring a somewhat similar way of accounting for group shifts, and at the same time to be relying increasingly on the structured group decision tasks that we have been describing in this section. Observe, too, that the norm-value hypothesis is, in a general way, not altogether inconsistent with the emphasis on outcome payoffs that Zajonc and his associates have emphasized. Both ideas focus on the content of the task and the individual's expectations about what is important; the social interaction subsequently acts upon these tendencies, though in a complex way, to produce shifts (if any are to be produced) in a particular direction.

Concluding remarks about individual and group risk taking. There are two particularly important conclusions to be drawn from the research dealing with risk taking in choice-dilemma and structured-task situations:

a)   The biasing or directing power of small groups has been brought out more forcefully in groups yielding a decision than in groups primarily concerned with learning or problem solving.

b)   Explanations about group performance that ignore the particular task-elicited behavior and the particular system of interpersonal relations that ultimately produce the group response to the task turn out to be inadequate descriptions of collective behavior. There are several kinds of tasks that by definition have something to do with risk. In the future we are likely to see not any single explanation of group shifts, but *several* explanations of group risk taking. After all, there are several ways in which risk can be associated with group life, including several tasks and social combination processes.

To the extent that the kinds of tasks discussed earlier have distinct real-life analogs, the practical implications of group risk taking are, of course, clear and powerful. As a final illustration of the practical implications of our discussion about group decisions, imagine that there exists a chief executive or leader of a large institution or nation. He seeks to make a wise decision reflecting the considered opinions or decision preferences of the population making up the institution. He cannot speak to everyone, but there exists a system whereby the whole population is assigned to groups, each of which yields a single decision after voting according to, say, a plurality rule. One representative from each group, in turn, meets with other similar representatives to form small groups operating on the same formal scheme. Each representative holds a preference selected by his earlier group. At this level, groups reach decisions and then select representatives precisely as before. The process then goes on for some number of levels until the final set of n groups make their decisions known to the chief executive. If the initial relative frequencies of preferences are the same for all alternatives, then the chief obtains an accurate appraisal of the population preference distribution from the distribution across the final set of groups. On the other hand, if this is not the case, and the population initially tends to prefer some alternatives to others, the final preference distribution across the final set of groups will underestimate the less frequent and overestimate the more frequent preferences in the original population distribution. That is to say, the initially frequent decisions become even more frequent in the end, and the less popular become even less popular yet. And this is solely the consequence of (a) the form of the original preference distribution and (b) the decision rule used to arrive at a group decision at each level.

The implications concerning the "accuracy" of an executive's information are quite obvious. Is this an approximation of the process used by a number of existing institutions in our culture? Perhaps it is. Of course, preference is not correctness, and a number of interpersonal influence processes are also likely to play a role in actual applications.

CHAPTER FOUR

Variables Affecting Group Performance

We began our discussion by considering the discrepancy between individual and group performance. We continued with an account of individual performance in a social context, and then proceeded to the more general question of how individuals combine their behaviors into a group product. So far, we have always been concerned in some way with the individual. However, most of the experimental research dealing with group performance has focused on the group itself as the object of study, without necessarily studying individual performance at the same time. It is therefore important to give some attention to those environmental and human qualities that might influence performance at the group level. We will sample some of this knowledge in the following sections.

GROUP SIZE

The variable of group size is in many ways similar to *time* treated as an independent variable. Time is sometimes said to have very little psychological effect other than to provide an opportunity for other variables to come into play. If group size increases, it is obvious that more persons are available for acquiring, processing, or recalling task-related information, and for developing ever more complex patterns of interpersonal relations. One kind of increase in *potential* group productivity is easily seen by assuming the now familiar Lorge-Solomon Model A: if the probability of solution for an individual is .25, the probability for a two-person group is .44, but the probability is .68 for a group of size four.

Where some heterogeneity of performance exists in the population, a larger group is more likely to represent the population accurately, regardless of "correctness" criteria. Moreover, if one recalls from our earlier discussions and from elementary statistics that the standard error of the mean is smaller than the standard deviation, he will see that, if the group product is an average, the larger group will yield a more stable estimate of the population average than a small group (see Steiner, 1966).

Aside from the increase in resources, an increase in size also brings with it greater opportunities for encountering an attractive companion with whom interaction is rewarding, and this may serve to keep an individual working in the group. Similarly, the opportunity to "hide in the crowd" or otherwise gain respite from the pressure of constant scrutiny or "being on stage" occurs more frequently in large than in small groups.

Disadvantages also accompany an increase in size, in that social obstacles (see Collins and Guetzkow, 1964) are increasingly evident. In order to make good use of the potential resources, more group effort must be devoted to the orderly formation of subgroups when the parent group is large. Subgroups may permit some of the intimate and efficient interaction that accomplishes the same or complementary work simultaneously at several different places in the group, and at the same time allow the larger group to achieve some of the social advantages of small groups. Splinter groups or subgroups tend to increase in number with group size, and a very important management problem is to prevent subgroups from having goals *inconsistent* with those of the larger group. The attempt to solve this problem often leads to the formation of traditional groups having formally *planned* subgroups or some kind of structural arrangement that allows the smaller groups to make a direct contribution to the overall aims.

While heterogeneity of composition in a large group may be desirable from one point of view, it also has its liabilities. In a very heterogeneous group the achievement of sufficient agreement for *any action at all* may be exceedingly difficult. This problem is especially troublesome if the group works according to a stringent decision scheme, such as achieving unanimity on some proposal.

In general, it appears that, as group size increases, contending forces are unleashed, some of which foster performance while others hinder it. A well-known study by Gibb (1951) is one of the few available that illustrate empirically the outcomes of these facilitating and inhibiting influences. Gibb observed groups ranging in size from "one" to 96 and found that the number of solutions produced for a problem-solving task was a negatively accelerating function of size. After each group discussed the task, it reported verbally to the experimenter the ideas for solution that had been generated. Although each larger group produced more ideas than the smaller, the increment in productivity was progressively smaller with each size increase. As was mentioned earlier in this book, when time for work is held constant and size increases there is progressively less opportunity per person to either discuss or make one's ideas known. Hence, it is difficult to use the increased potential of the group in any effective way, unless a compensating interpersonal organization or structure is achieved.

However, there is reason to believe that size-related changes in internal social processes also contribute in another way to the resource-utilization problem in larger groups. For example, Gibb also reported that a higher proportion of members experienced *feelings of inhibition* about participating as group size increased, and that increasing the formality of the group work setting also increased these feelings against participation. Such feelings apparently pass into behavior, for there is ample evidence that the *disparity* among the discussion participation rates of the members increases with group size (Bales, Strodtbeck, Mills, and Roseborough, 1951; Stephan and Mishler, 1952). If persons are added to a group that has been interacting, the original, frequent contributors increase their participation and undercontributors decrease their participation even further. Moreover, the average group member apparently values more the *opportunity* to participate than actual participation in group discussion (Marquis, Guetzkow, and Heyns, 1951). Satisfaction with the group discussion, however, is greater if one does speak, even though his ideas are not accepted or included in the final group product.

We thus see that the changes in personal and interpersonal processes that occur with an increase in group size have primarily negative implications for performance—in spite of positive returns to be expected from an increase in potential resources. One source of these size-dependent attitudinal or morale changes may simply be the difficulties associated with increased physical distance. Without some degree of physical proximity, the achievement of effective communication or intimate social exchange may represent a serious problem. There even appear to be customary distances between interactors, and when these are violated discomfort may ensue. The customary distance between two persons may vary from culture to culture, or from situation to situation within a culture. In any event, it appears that a number of features of "group geography" have an important effect on such developments as the emergence of leaders or the evolution of interaction patterns (see Sommer, 1959, 1961, 1962).

Eye Contact

Not the least of the advantages of close proximity to one's companion and easy access to his attention is the easy exchange of nonverbal information in conjunction with regular conversation. The large group makes such informal exchange very difficult. Several investigators (e.g., Argyle, 1967) have discovered that eye movement, direction of gaze, and mutual "eye contact" serve important interaction scheduling functions. The members of an interacting pair tend to scan each other's face, but the main target of the gaze is the eyes. On the average, about 30 to 60 percent of the time is spent in eye contact, and from 10 to 30 percent of this is mutual contact, lasting usually about one second at a time. The speaker initially begins his speech looking away from the target, but at the ends of phrases or such units he tends to gaze briefly at the other's eyes; the end of the speech is signaled by a rather long gaze. More looking takes place while listening than while speaking. Conversation is apparently scheduled in part by such intermittent gazes of various durations.

Looking at another has been further summarized by Argyle as a social technique or nonverbal signaling system.

a)   A looker may invite interaction by staring at another person who is on the other side of a room. The target's studied return of the gaze is generally interpreted as acceptance of the invitation, while averting the eyes is a rejection of the looker's request.

b)   There is more mutual eye contact between friends than others, and a looker's frank gaze is widely interpreted as positive regard.

c)   Persons who seek eye contact while speaking are regarded not only as exceptionally well-disposed by their target, but also as more believable and earnest.

d)   If the usual short, intermittent gazes during conversation are replaced by gazes of longer duration, the target interprets this as meaning that the task is less important than the personal relation between the two persons.

There are several methodological difficulties associated with the measurement of eye-contact variables, but this summary serves to illustrate the general findings. It is easy to see that eye contact and the resulting interaction scheduling should proceed more easily in a small group than in a large one. It is also easy to imagine how eye-contact phenomena work to aid the formation of pairs and triads in a crowded room. An invitation to a corner tête-a-tête may be more easily accomplished by eye than by voice.

GROUP COMPOSITION

For the student of group performance and the layman alike, one of the most appealing questions concerning group products concerns the relationship between output and the *kind* of persons responsible for that output. Internal group processes, social structure, and task variables have a place, but surely the talents and personalities of the members should be assessed *directly* if one wishes to predict group performance accurately. Intuitively, it seems that social process as well as task performance should be heavily dependent on the members' personalities. We will consider later the problems associated with the *in situ* measurement of interaction, but at this point we might inquire about the prediction of group performance from prediscussion assessment of individual members.

Unfortunately, there is scarcely a question dealing with group behavior that is less easily answered in a forthright way than that concerning the composition-performance relationship. We might mention at the outset that this state of affairs is due to three problems: (a) difficulties associated with the measurement of some personal attributes, (b) unique or rare influences that arise from "accidental" events occurring during the interaction itself, and (c) the difficulties associated with describing the task output in an orderly way—a problem we have described before as the task taxonomy problem.

It is useful to distinguish between, on the one hand, task-related intellective abilities or skills and, on the other, personality traits (extroversion, dominance, authoritarianism, etc.). The latter are perhaps less directly related to task performance *per se* than to interpersonal processes ultimately responsible for group work. The extremes are obvious; five morons are unlikely to outperform five persons of evident brilliance, and five dedicated enemies are unlikely to outperform five friends on a problem requiring cooperative solution. As we move to group compositions that are less extreme or include different *patterns* of individual differences, the prediction problem becomes more troublesome.

Intellective Abilities and Performance

Considering intellective abilities first, we find that both general (intelligence) and specific abilities of members (measured by standard tests of intellective abilities) are consistently related to total group performance. However, the relationship is typically far from perfect, and is often surprisingly low—apparently moderated by nonintellective influences arising during interaction (see Mann, 1959; Heslin, 1964). Although the use of psychological tests to measure component abilities in task performances is not without merit, the use of individual task behavior to predict subsequent group task behavior results in even better predictions, and this latter strategy appears to be the more efficient. In a sense, we have already considered the prediction question at some length. From our discussion of individual-group comparisons, it should be evident that a knowledge of how individual persons attack a task is insufficient to predict group performance unless allowance is made in the prediction process for socially induced individual changes (such as social facilitation or inhibition) and for the way in which individual contributions are combined through interaction.

Olson and Davis (1964) administered to coacting individuals a parallel form of the problem (a set of simple arithmetic problems) subsequently attacked by the same subjects in four-person groups. Pretesting permitted the sorting of subjects into "probable solvers" and "probable nonsolvers." Olson and Davis found that predictions of group success were little better than those achieved without knowledge of the two ability levels from pretesting.

A somewhat similar approach was taken by Johnson and Torcivia (1967), who administered a simple mathematical puzzle to a large number of individuals. Some subjects were subsequently paired and worked on the problem again, while others continued to work alone at the second testing. The pairs were comprised of subjects who were initially either both right, mixed (one right and one wrong), both wrong with similar initial answers, or both wrong with dissimilar initial answers. "Both-right" pairs did not decrease in performance, and "both-wrong" pairs did not improve. Moreover, the fact that "both-wrong-with-dissimilar-initial-answers" pairs did not improve suggests that simple group heterogeneity (relative to the task) does not itself facilitate performance. The most interesting results came from the mixed pairs, in which one member was initially right and one wrong. The "right-wrong" pairs were better than initially wrong individuals who worked a second time, and worse than similar initially correct individuals. However, the direction of change in the "right-wrong" pairs could be predicted with some accuracy by using information on which member of the pair was more certain of his initial answer. (The subjects had not only recorded their initial answers, but they had also rated them as to their own certainty about correctness.)

Thus apparently the personal conviction interacted with discussion in determining how the conflict in member predispositions would be resolved. It is, of course, just this kind of personal-social data that is usually lacking and always difficult to obtain during interaction, especially in larger groups. Thus the initial distribution of member abilities or performance must, if it is to prove helpful, be supplemented by some idea about the interaction pattern that is likely to ensue.

Personality Traits of Group Members

We will concentrate on the pregroup measurement of traits in the hope of relating such data to ultimate group performance. There are several recent reviews of the existing knowledge in this area which are addressed directly to the point we are considering (Mann, 1959; Heslin, 1964; McGrath and Altman, 1966). Aside from intellective abilities, traits that have been especially considered are general adjustment, extroversion-introversion, dominance, masculinity-feminity, conservatism, interpersonal sensitivity, and authoritarianism. Despite an occasional report to the contrary, the general finding appears to be that personality measures are neither *strongly* nor *consistently* related to group performance *per se*, with the possible exception of adjustment (which is an ambiguous label anyway).

What is the reason for these disappointing results? A major part of the difficulty would appear to be that the very expectation of a *direct* relationship between personality and performance is naive, despite its popularity over many years. McGrath and Altman (1966, pp. 64-65) have summarized the matter this way:

> ... results are equivocal regarding the effects of personality-social factors on individual and group performance; this equivocation is somewhat in contrast to the attention such variables have received by researchers and consumers. ... It may be that the confused results are due to a methodological problem. For example, in aptitude and ability measurement, psychologists have well-developed tools whereas in the measurement of personality, attitudes, and group cohesion our measurement technology is less advanced.
>
> On the other hand, consider the role of these variables from a conceptual point of view. When we speak of abilities and experience as determinants of performance, we are usually presuming that the more of the characteristic the better, and this usually is true. However, for personal-social variables this monotonic principle may not apply; rather, we may be in a realm where either *too much or too little* of a characteristic interfered with performance, with some optimum, in-between point enhancing performance. ...
> Perhaps individual and group abilities and experience tend to set limits within which the group can function just as intelligence may have limits set by heredity. In the same way that the environment may only exert an influence within the fixed bounds of intellectual capacity, so may it be that social-personal variables can enhance group performance only within limits set by abilities, training, and experience. ... We need a better understanding of the sequential linkages that begin with inputs in the form of member, group, and task characteristics, that become *manifested in* intermediate interactive processes, and that culminate in a performance output. ...
> We need a more sensitive appreciation of the parameters and properties of different types of performance. It is oversimplifying to group all types of performance under a single heading. There must be a better appreciation of what the varieties of performance are and a better appreciation of differences in performance across situations and tasks. Behavior does not occur in a vacuum; it results from an interaction of behavior, situation, and task.

In summary, it is perhaps not too surprising that pregroup measurements of personality and abilities have the marginal status that they now do in the prediction of group performance. A careful perusal of the names of personality traits suggests that these concepts have *social behavior* as referents, not intellective or motor behaviors. Dominance or extroversion, for example, imply the existence of another person or persons. Thus we would expect personality factors to be directly related to the social milieu, and group output only derivatively and in some complex way. We might close by noting, parenthetically, that traditional measures of personality traits (self-report questionnaires and the like) have rarely been validated against actual social behavior, despite the implications derivable from the trait names. A more sophisticated use of personality traits in the study of group-based social behavior will probably have to await the establishment of predictive validity for personality assessment tools.

GROUP COHESIVENESS

Some groups, whether in the laboratory or in real life, seem to possess a certain atmosphere of "closeness" or commonness of purpose that is lacking in other groups. Such a quality may seem self-evident to the social essayist or passing observer. But does such a concept have a clear, concrete referent of the kind required by the student of social behavior? Moreover, if such a "spirit" actually exists in the world of groups, does it influence group performance in a definite and orderly way? The label that has come to include most of the ideas expressed above is group *cohesiveness*. Although variously defined over the years, cohesiveness is generally regarded as characteristic of the group in which the forces acting on the members to remain in the group are greater than the total forces acting on them to leave it. Cohesive groups, then, are collectivities in which interpersonal attraction or the yen for mutual association is high; groups of low cohesiveness are, in the extreme, groups that are breaking up—going out of recognizable existence. The definition suggests that group cohesiveness is a matter of degree and emphasizes the dynamic nature of the relationship among the members.

A very large number of sources of attraction to a group are conceivable, but in practice they may be grouped into two categories (Cartwright and Zander, 1968):

a) The group members themselves are attractive in that the individual enjoys interacting with them, receiving their support on some issue or issues, or in general wishes to enter into some kind of exchange relationship with one or more of them.

b) The goals or exterior tasks confronting the group are consistent with those of the individual person, and can best be handled by group action.

In both cases there are a number of variables that increase the attractiveness of the group, but all of them have the feature that they increase the satisfaction of the individual's needs through association with the group.

The Effects of Cohesiveness on Performance

Since cohesive groups are composed of persons motivated to be together, we would expect group performance to benefit from cohesiveness through general motivation alone. Recall that if the probability of achieving a group goal is constant per unit time, then the longer a group remains together and at the task, the higher the total probability of success. While this must surely be a major advantage of group work over solitary work, we should recall, too, that a high level of arousal can actually interfere with some tasks. To the extent that cohesiveness means proximity and distracting interaction, group cohesiveness can contribute to a reduced likelihood of successful goal attainment. As is the case with so many other variables, the *task* must be considered in any prediction of the specific effects of cohesiveness on group success.

Cohesive groups possess the advantage of mutual availability of the members. That is to say, the willingness to interact has the potential advantage of making group resources available to a degree that the less cohesive group may not enjoy. Again, this advantage must be tempered by the frequent finding that the pleasure from interaction itself, in cohesive groups, sometimes exceeds the task-specific motivation, and greater energy is devoted to interpersonal relations than to overcoming the task obstacles. Hence, performance suffers.

One way in which this is especially likely to happen is illustrated by the finding that an increase in cohesiveness results in an increase in pressures to uniformity (Back, 1951). If uniformity of response can be achieved more easily on a wrong or low-quality response, overall performance will decline while satisfactory interpersonal relations may be preserved. For example, Schachter, Ellertson, McBride, and Gregory (1951) and Berkowitz (1954) found that highly cohesive groups were more likely to accept or agree upon a *common* group goal than were groups low in cohesiveness, regardless of whether the goal represented a high or low rate of production.

The Effects of Performance on Cohesiveness: A Cycle

For those tasks that permit feedback on progress, cohesiveness may produce a cyclic effect. It is often said about real-life groups that there is nothing like success to increase morale or group spirit. A near universal finding is that cohesiveness generally increases with success.

That success has the effect of increasing cohesiveness is illustrated in a famous study by Sherif and Sherif (1953), in which boys at a summer camp were first permitted to form freely in informal groups as they became acquainted. Subsequently they were placed in groups in which their friends (as revealed by earlier questionnaires) constituted only about one-third of the membership. At the end of five days, during which each group shared many pleasant experiences, a second questionnaire revealed that the friendship patterns had shifted so as to reflect the membership of the final group, and that these groups were highly cohesive. Cohesiveness could, in theory, thus be manipulated by a careful scheduling of success-failure experiences. In general, task failure or imperfect goal attainment tends to lower cohesiveness and thus break the performance-cohesiveness cycle (or perhaps initiate a reverse failure-low cohesiveness cycle).

Even the *method of attack* on the task can be a source of disagreement that lowers the level of interpersonal attraction. For example, when disagreement exists about the best means of constructing a solution to a problem, the result is a lowering of cohesiveness (Raven and Rietsema, 1957; French, 1941), sometimes to the point where members leave before a final product is proposed at all.

Interestingly enough, there are instances in which task failure does not result in a lowering of cohesiveness, but on the contrary may even result in its *increase*. One important case is that in which group failure can be attributed to an external threat or malevolent agency. In such cases group failure may be a special boon for flagging interest in the group. There are other exceptions as well (see Festinger, Riecken, and Schachter, 1956), but we shall not consider their peculiar significance at this time.

Another concept that has been considered rather similar to cohesiveness, in that it likewise focuses on the nature of the interdependence among group members, is that of cooperation-competition. This topic, to which we now turn, has a particular appeal in our culture.

Cooperation and Competition

Intergroup competition generally tends to increase cohesiveness within a group, while *intragroup* competition tends to decrease it. Deutsch (1968) has in fact demonstrated, both theoretically and empirically, that group members who are cooperatively interdependent in the service of some task tend to be friendlier and mutually more influential, and otherwise give evidence of higher cohesiveness, than do similar groups acting in a competitive manner.

We might ask at this point just what it is that affects or controls the emergence of a cooperative, as opposed to a competitive, style of interaction. Because of practical implications, the question is often given the form: "Which is superior in terms of performance—cooperation or competition?" This question is, of course, naive in much the same way as the question about individual or group superiority considered earlier. One may well choose to compete with others because he dislikes them, desires to appear in a certain light, or is responding to motives unconnected with the immediate task and interaction sequence. We should not forget that cooperation, like cohesiveness, is more accurately described as the name of a *class* of phenomena. Many behaviors are cooperative in one setting, but meaningless in another.

Most of our discussion about group performance has carried, at least implicitly, the assumption of a cooperative group. Any competitive behavior that arose was more a function of "interaction accidents" than of instructions from an experimenter or demands of the task. Aside from these interpersonal variables, there are, however, conditions associated with the task that foster cooperative or competitive behavior.

Let us consider the question of payoff or feedback associated with the quality of performance. If the task permits individual contributions to be recovered or graded in the final group product, then *individual members* may be selectively rewarded accordingly. Alternatively, the group may be paid off *as a whole*. The result, not very surprisingly, is that cooperative behavior is usually evident in the latter kind of group, while a competitive interaction style typically characterizes the former sort of group. Deutsch (1949) used these two kinds of payoff as a means of creating internally cooperative and competitive small groups that were required, over the course of several weeks, to work at a sequence of human relations problems and logical puzzles. He found a higher degree of productivity in cooperative groups: higher output of puzzle solutions per unit of time and a higher quality of proposals for the human relations problems. This performance elevation was apparently achieved by means of pressures toward productive work in the cooperative groups; these groups coordinated the division of labor and achieved better communication among members in order to utilize available resources. Observers also judged cooperative groups to invest more effort in maintenance, strengthening, or regulation of the group. Such pressures to attend to group-centered activities had the effect not only of increasing cohesiveness, but also of keeping the group functioning smoothly and productively.

The performance virtues of cooperative functioning, evident from this study, do not apply to all settings and tasks. The Deutsch investigation was centered at the group level, and some tasks, as we know from earlier sections on individual-group comparisons, are more efficiently attacked by isolated individuals. Competition, if not overwhelming, may actually foster helpful isolation while keeping motivation at a suitably high level; in this case the effects of cooperation and competition as described above might be reversed.

The possible variations on the cooperation-competition paradigm are numerous, especially if the many qualifying variables are taken into account. But we can see from Deutsch's account some of the ways in which cooperation affects interaction and ultimately group performance.

A second kind of task-group format in which the structure of the task and the accompanying social structure combine to intensify the interpersonal confrontation is illustrated by *bargaining situations.* Cooperation effects, like so many other interaction variables, are frequently difficult to study in a precise way at the level of four- or five-person groups. By focusing on a task that is cast as a game between two or more players (or between two or more teams), a more detailed study of mutual conflict and the manner of its resolution (cooperation, competition, withdrawal, etc.) is possible.

We shall not consider further these interdependence problems, but shall instead direct the reader to Gergen's (1969) thorough discussion of such behavior-exchange situations.

NORMS

The final group-level concept that we shall consider is that of *norm*. Few concepts in social psychology have figured more prominently in explanations of collective behavior than has the idea of a social norm. It is thus somewhat surprising that it has so infrequently been treated directly as an independent or dependent variable in experimental studies of group performance. In its most general sense, a norm is a standard against which the appropriateness of a behavior is to be judged. Some norms are pervasive, in that they are widely shared by the bulk of the members of a culture; others are local, in the sense that they apply specifically to the members of a particular group.

Norms vary in a number of respects. Some norms (perhaps most) apply to overt behavior, while others seem to guide subjective states when the individual is faced with uncertainty. Some norms are formal, in that they are written or otherwise conspicuously and intentionally adopted by a group (rules or operating procedures). On the other hand, many norms are informal in their origin; they arise from the interaction of the group members over time. Working norms emerging in this way may even occasionally be in conflict with the formal group norms which ostensibly govern behavior in some particular case. Informal norms are not necessarily equally evident to all group members; but in most small groups that have existed for a time, there is little likelihood that norm violations occur frequently without the awareness of most of the members.

It is generally thought that long-term groups are more likely to display distinct norms than are the short-term groups typical of laboratory experiments on group performance. This is probably true, but some group norms have their origin less in the immediate performance-oriented interaction than in some *value*—a basic belief or assumption about what is good, right, or proper. The norm in this sense is a kind of "logical" consequence of a value that is shared by the members of an *ad hoc* group, who after all come from a common culture.

However, there is reason to believe that group norms do arise over a rather short time period. But just how rapidly and under what conditions do norms form—norms that are strong enough to guide behavior to a significant degree? This is a question that remains to be systematically explored. Most of the available experimental evidence on the way norms function in social behavior comes from studies of social conformity and interpersonal influence, where norms obviously play an important role (see Kiesler and Kiesler, 1969). We shall at this point consider only one line of evidence on the rapid evolution of a norm and its effects on individual performance— namely, the evidence concerning judgment tasks.

Sherif (1936) set out to determine whether, and how, a set of individuals would develop a common standard when faced with a judgment task that precluded the easy use of external, physical standards. The task made use of the *autokinetic effect,* which was known even before the rise of experimental psychology. A stationary point of light in a suitably darkened room appears to move, and a subject unaware of the actual physical situation is easily induced to estimate the extent of this movement. Sherif required some subjects to judge the distance the light moved while they were alone in the room, and others to do likewise in the presence of other judges (i.e., in a group). In some cases the individual subjects had judged in a group situation prior to performing alone; other subjects were inexperienced. Sherif found that the inexperienced individuals soon developed a reference point about which the light seemed to range in a consistent manner, and that this norm was peculiar to the individual subject, persisting without much change over time. When subjects who had established their personal norms in this way were grouped, and then continued to make judgments in each other's presence, the previously established standards began to converge. The convergence took place without any related conversation or formal decision by the group as to how the members should judge the movement. The experimental paradigm is thus the same as that for the coaction studies we discussed earlier, but in this case the nature of the coactors' performance is especially evident to the others.

When subjects made their first judgments in the presence of a group, Sherif found the convergence to a collective norm to be even more rapid. Moreover, the group norm was pervasive in individual judgments. When subjects with experience in a group subsequently made a series of judgments alone, the *group* norm was "carried along," for the new judgments by individuals complied with the norms of the previous membership group.

We shall not explore the many interesting properties of norms, but rather concentrate on the implications for performance. The focus of the norm is either (a) *direct,* in that group output (quality, rate, etc.) is itself regulated by the norm, or (b) *indirect,* in that interpersonal behavior is generally affected and task performance is derivatively dependent on that interaction. In either case, there are two major components of a norm whereby the regulatory function is carried out: (a) the *behavioral expectation* or *point of maximum appropriateness* along the behavioral continuum; and (b) the *limits of tolerable deviations* about this expectation. When the behavior to which the norm is applicable deviates "too far" in any direction, the deviant may expect negative sanctions (rejections, penalties, or disapproval). Although sometimes there may be *distinct* limits, as with formal norms, in practice it would seem that the deviations about the expected behavior are increasingly likely to incur some expression of group displeasure as they become more extreme. The severity of the negative sanctions may even be roughly proportional to the size of the deviation. Conversely, behaviors along the continuum that approach the expectation are increasingly likely to receive positive sanctions such as praise and other expressions of approval, although both negative and positive sanctions are in many cases quite subtle.

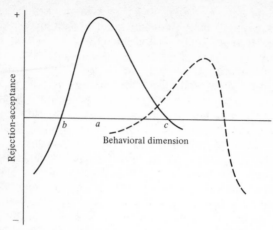

Fig. 4.1   Graphs describing the structure of two different norms.

There are two further important components to the conception of norms as described here: (a) *intensity* of approval or disapproval and (b) *probability* of that approval or disapproval being overtly expressed by others. The latter component is especially noteworthy because such social expression is a function of more than simply extremity of deviation.

The ideas just expressed are rather similar to those of Jackson (1965), who has emphasized the structural qualities of norms. These notions are further illustrated by the graph in Fig. 4.1. Jackson calls such a graph the *return potential curve.* The horizontal axis is any well-defined behavioral dimension, and the vertical axis is the degree of acceptance-rejection accorded the behavior. Imagine that the behavioral dimension is "amount of discussion participation." The solid curve implies that those individuals who talk an amount *a* receive maximum approval. However, a group member deviating as much as *b* in one direction or *c* in the other has exceeded the indifference points, and some form of social disapproval is likely to follow such excesses. The dashed line might represent a group having a different norm structure, or the same group under different circumstances. Observe that the two curves differ in maximum height, location along the horizontal axis, and general shape. There is no reason why norms need to be symmetric, or to have the same structure from one behavior to the next. Nevertheless, the structures of various norms have not yet been determined empirically, and the consequences of various group or individual norm structures for group performance have yet to be explored.

The chief advantage of conceiving of norms in this structural fashion is that a number of properties may be easily deduced. (You may wish to try this as an exercise.) Some precision is thereby given to the norm concept, and comparisons across groups, places, or times are facilitated. We will consider first some of Jackson's findings with regard to widely shared norms. Then we shall take up some examples showing the effect of norms on interpersonal behavior and group performance.

Jackson (1965), in a study of oil refinery executives, required the executives to rate each of a set of ordered behaviors along a continuum of approval-disapproval; the averaged ratings yielded return potential curves of the type represented by the graphs in Fig. 4.1. Jackson found that men with specialized or professional training gave return potential curves (mean ratings) about which the ratings were much less variable than were the ratings of executives with equal status but nontechnical backgrounds about *their* return potential curves. Jackson interpreted such differences in rating variability to indicate a lack of norm crystallization for those with non-technical training. This study, along with others, suggests how the same behavior may be governed by different norms in different populations. Hence, different interaction styles and consequent variations in performance might be anticipated from groups coming from different populations. Indeed, outright norm conflict might be anticipated for mixed-norm groups.

It is easy to imagine from Sherif's work how norms act directly in setting productivity standards for group output, and we shall therefore mention only briefly one common kind of situation. Small groups having a specific but collective responsibility for work occur often as part of a production line or as maintenance crews. Although a company may formally set an expected standard of productivity, and may even set the lower bounds, it is often an informal norm of the work group that sets upper bounds on group or individual output. Members who "overproduce" in comparison to the group's informally established norm are informed (this process is called "norm sending" by Rommetveit, 1955) in a number of ways about the unsuitability of their deviation (Roethlisberger and Dickson, 1939). Among the common norm-sending techniques are the labeling of overproducers with derogatory nicknames, and making them the butt of sarcastic remarks during work.

Members may deviate from group norms in some interpersonal activity not directly related to performance, but rejection is more serious if the deviation is relevant to or has implications for group goals. Evidence for the way group members react to task-relevant and task-irrelevant deviation comes from a study by Schachter (1951). Schachter recruited subjects under the guise of setting up case-study, editorial, movie, and radio clubs. Cohesiveness was manipulated by assigning some subjects to their preferred topic group (high cohesiveness) and others to a nonpreferred group (low cohesiveness). At some point, all groups received a case summary of a juvenile delinquent named Johnny Rocco, and were required to discuss and rate the kind of treatment he should receive. The group members could select from among seven proposed treatments that ranged from rather severe to fairly lenient. For the case-study and editorial groups, the Rocco case was relevant to their purpose or overall goals as explained by the experimenter, but it was a "side issue" for the camera and radio clubs. Thus group cohesiveness and task relevance were two independent variables examined simultaneously. In all groups the experimenter planted three confederates who interacted in specific ways with the five to seven naive subjects comprising the remainder of the group. First, the deviant and another confederate known as a "slider" took the position of extreme punishment, while a third confederate took the position that had been most frequently advocated by the naive subjects during a prediscussion opinion rating of the treatment to be accorded Johnny Rocco. The slider gradually changed during discussion to the most popular position in the group, but the deviant continued to defend his extremely harsh recommendation.

The most striking evidence concerning the reaction to the three confederates came in post-discussion interpersonal ratings of who should be included in later group meetings of a smaller size, and in nominations for group duties (committees) planned for a later time. The results were very clear. In their interpersonal ratings, all groups tended to reject most strongly the deviant, next most strongly the slider, and then the confederate advocating the popular position. Moreover, the deviant was heavily undernominated for the most important group committees and overnominated for the least important committees. Finally, it was generally found that deviant rejection of this sort was greatest in cohesive, task-relevant groups.

Communication data obtained from tabulating discussion-rate and interaction patterns were less decisive. However, groups high in both cohesiveness and task relevance did tend to direct less discussion toward the deviate as the session wore on.

What are the implications for group performance of "redefining" group boundaries to exclude to some degree a norm-violating member or members? The most obvious effect is to preserve the group so that it can go about its business. Of course, this assumes that the *potential task contributions* of the rejected members do not outweigh their liabilities as a disrupting influence on group processes.

Thus the major effect of isolating or neutralizing a deviant depends on his potential contribution to the group task, and on how, if at all, this can be adjusted when desirable for group performance. The Schachter study gives a clear indication of how groups react to deviants—even groups that have had no long and intimate history.

CONCLUDING REMARKS
CONCERNING GROUP PERFORMANCE VARIABLES

An organizing theme throughout this book has been the comparison of individuals with groups in various circumstances of performance. In particular, we have taken the position that the translation of individual task behavior into group performance is an important aim of social theory and research. However, some phenomena associated with performing groups lend themselves to analysis into individual member contributions, both conceptual and experimental, less easily than others. This chapter has dealt with some of these important but "resistant" phenomena. One of these phenomena, cohesiveness, is primarily a state of groups, and it is difficult to define an analogous state in the single individual. Of course, even such group-level concepts as cohesiveness can conceivably exist as *propensities* or *tendencies* in individual subjects, but the empirical transition has not been especially successful—particularly in view of the amount of attention that has been devoted to the problem.

CHAPTER FIVE

Group Structure and Performance

Social interaction tends to develop along certain lines or paths. Just as a road map indicates the highways connecting cities, so can one construct a picture of social interaction that reflects the pattern of exchanges among persons in a collectivity. The pattern of interpersonal relations is called *group structure.* In this sense, structure is a picture of interpersonal processes taken at a particular point in time. A particular structure may be relatively enduring or emerge only briefly, depending on a number of factors such as task demands, physical surroundings, motivation, and the life expectancy of the group. Long-term groups are obviously the sort most likely to yield a well-defined structure, but even the *ad hoc* group typical of the laboratory ordinarily displays a detectable structure that is an important determinant of performance.

One strategy for the study of group structure under controlled conditions is to *impose* a structure upon a small group. Structure is thus treated as an independent variable, and the consequences of a particular structure may be observed with regard to group performance, interpersonal responses, and the personal reactions of members. A second strategy is to regard group structure as an *emergent* phenomenon—the interpersonal consequence of a set of persons interacting over a period of time. Group structure is thus regarded as a dependent variable. In either case, the concept is essentially the same and the notion of group structure is one of the important mediators between individual input and group output.

Sometimes imposed structures are called *formal* and emergent structures are labeled *informal.* Of course, the newcomer to an established group may find the distinction trivial, for he faces an existing organization of persons whose conduct is already governed to some degree by norms, patterns of interpersonal behavior, and the task developed in the group. Most of us have at some time been confronted with the problem of learning the structure in a group that we have joined. Although the new member is not likely to develop the same abstract picture that the student of social behavior uses, we can still inquire as to the features of structure that affect him and with which he must come to terms. Before exploring further the role of structure, we should consider the nature of the concept in more detail.

THE REPRESENTATION OF STRUCTURE

The elements of structure have traditionally been known as *positions.* Each position usually has one or more *roles* associated with it, and different role-positions may have different degrees of accompanying status (prestige or importance accorded by the group). A role is a set of behaviors that are expected of, or characteristically displayed by, the person occupying a particular position. The individual holding a position may play his roles in an idiosyncratic fashion, or sometimes create new ones. But if the position possesses well-defined roles at all, he must meet at least some criteria for executing his roles if he is to function satisfactorily in that position. There is a bewildering array of definitions of the key notions of *position, role, status,* and *connections among positions,* for these ideas have long been employed by different writers in sociology, anthropology, and social psychology. This state of affairs has led many theorists, especially those favoring an abstract mathematical treatment of structure, to regard structure simply as a *set of elements* among which there exists a *well-defined relation;* the elements and associated relations may be represented by a *graph* consisting of points and lines, respectively.

The geometrical quality of structure is easily grasped by considering the different structures represented by the different graphs of Fig. 5.1. Graph (a) appears to be a chain and, to many persons, the top-to-bottom arrangement implies a kind of superiority-inferiority relationship among elements. In (b), position *A* similarly appears to be dominant and at the same time to be "central" in the sense that *A* is related to all other positions, but no other position is related to any other except through *A*. In graph (c) the centrality of *A* is retained, but this graph does not suggest to most observers a "superiority" relation for *A*. However, the relationship among points in (b) and (c) is in fact identical. It is the spatial arrangement of the points that gives the different impressions. Observe the "circle" in (d) and how similar it is in general arrangement to (e), except for the *number* of connections per position. Both (d) and (e) imply a kind of "equalitarianism"; yet the two must surely differ psychologically, for in (d) each person is connected with only two others, while in (e) everyone is connected with everyone else.

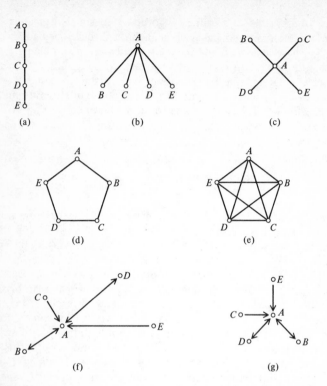

Fig. 5.1 Examples of graphs associated with various possible structures for five-person groups.

Finally, in graphs (f) and (g) we see that arrows, rather than lines, connect points. Between some positions, the relation appears to be two-way (e.g., between *A* and *D*), while for others the relation is in one direction only. Moreover, (f) and (g) are identical except for the spatial arrangement of positions and the *length* of the connecting lines.

The advantages of such pictures are obviously due to their convenience as an aid to intuition. However, the disadvantages should be obvious. Although helpful rules exist, it is very difficult to draw diagrams that do not convey an impression, perhaps not intended, about the nature of some structure; such an impression may be conveyed merely by the way physical distances, page placement, and the like are handled. In addition, it is not possible to operate mathematically upon diagrams in the way we have come to do with test scores or other measurements.

Sociomatrices

Empirical observations of interpersonal relations were once represented solely by diagrams, similar to those in Fig. 5.1, called *sociograms.* However,

Receiver

	A	B	C	D	E
A		1	0	1	0
B	1		0	0	0
C	1	0		0	0
D	1	0	0		0
E	1	0	0	0	

(Initiator)

Fig. 5.2 The sociomatrix (sometimes called the adjacency matrix) of graphs (f) and (g) in Fig. 5.1.

as group size increases, the confusion created by many points and lines, as well as a "fair" spatial arrangement, becomes intolerable. (Rules to minimize such difficulties are described by Proctor and Loomis, 1951; and Borgatta, 1951.) One alternative to sociograms is to employ matrices (called sociomatrices in this context) and sacrifice the intuitive advantages of sociograms for precision in representation and mathematical convenience. A sociomatrix is given in Fig. 5.2. The rows represent the sender or initiator of a social act, while the columns represent the receiver. The entry within each cell is either a one or a zero, representing either the presence or absence of a relation. Moreover, inspection of the sociomatrix indicates whether the relation is mutual or in one direction only. Every graph can be represented by a sociomatrix, and thus graphs are said to be isomorphic with sociomatrices. In fact, Fig. 5.2 is the matrix representation of graphs (f) and (g) in Fig. 5.1.

Sociomatrices not only have the advantage of precision in representation, but they also permit a number of analytical operations that sometimes reveal previously unsuspected implicit relationships among persons. In addition to absence, presence, and direction of a relation, the sociomatrix allows, in a straightforward way, the representation of the *strength* or *frequency* of a relation. In the latter case, the entries may accordingly take

	A	B	C	D	Sum	Relative frequency
A	0	25	24	16	65	.451
B	4	0	8	2	14	.097
C	24	9	0	22	55	.382
D	4	4	2	0	10	.069
Sum	32	38	34	40	144	
Relative frequency	.222	.264	.236	.278		

Fig. 5.3 A sociomatrix in which the entries represent the frequency of interpersonal communication.

values other than zero and one. The limitations here stem only from the kind and sophistication of the measurements. For example, the entries in the matrix displayed in Fig. 5.3 might indicate the empirically determined frequencies with which the persons arrayed along the rows communicate with those along the columns.

The preceding discussion has served to introduce the ideas of graphs and sociomatrices. The major value of sociomatrices for representing and analyzing structure, however, comes from their susceptibility to further mathematical treatment. Unfortunately, a discussion of the mathematical operations with sociomatrices is beyond the scope of this book (see Glanzer and Glaser, 1959, 1961; Flament, 1963; Davis, 1963; Harary, Norman, and Cartwright, 1965; Lindzey and Byrne, 1968).

Relations

In our concentration on the geometry of structure and its representation, we have neglected its substance: the *person* occupying a position and the *kind* of relation among positions. We now shall briefly consider the idea of a relation.

From one point of view, there are as many possible social relations as there are ways to describe sensibly how one person acts toward another. Consequently, a group possesses not one structure, but many. The structure of an existing group depends partly on which variable the investigator uses to differentiate it—that is to say, the particular relation in question. Thus, in a group performing a task, one structure may suffice for describing the pattern of friendship that develops, but a different structure may be required for describing the communication connections. A third graph might even be required in order to depict accurately the fact that some members have power over others in the process of actually deciding what the product of the group will finally be. We might expect such structures to be correlated, but rarely to overlap perfectly.

In principle, different relations may yield different structures. Some of the most common relations are dominance, communication, friendship, and influence. Deciding on a "true" list of possible structures is rather like deciding just how many personality traits are to be found in the adult human. At present, the selection of relations, like that of traits, depends on the individual investigator and the concepts relevant to the theory involved in a particular study. In other words, there is no universally accepted "stopping rule" for extracting structures. In any event, the notion of structure applies equally to all relations; and their representation, as in a sociomatrix, is similar.

As implied earlier, the structure-defining sociomatrix may refer to the *a priori permissible* relations, established by a formal structure, or it may be the summary of the pattern and strength of the relations that actually arose in a working group. Thus the rows in Fig. 5.2 may be interpreted as indicating that *A can* communicate with *B* and *D*, but no others; *B* can communicate with *A*, but no others, etc. Figure 5.3, on the other hand, might reflect the frequency of communication actually observed in a different group, and a row or column total would indicate a member's sending and receiving frequencies, respectively: *A* spoke a total of 65 times, and spoke to *B* and *C* about equally often (25 and 24), but somewhat less to *D* (16).

We shall consider only imposed structures in this chapter, for we lack the space here to review the findings on how emergent structures are related to group performance. A number of fascinating measurement problems exist concerning how self-reports are used to reconstruct the system of interpersonal relations; such self-reports may take the form of questionnaires or interviews in which a variety of questions are posed to obtain information on slightly different versions of a relation. Similarly, techniques for observing (by a trained judge) interpersonal activity concerning some relation are more easily conceived than practiced. Measurement problems notwithstanding, there is indeed a large literature dealing with recovering group structure from independent observations and interpersonal choices of work companions, friends, respected coworkers, and the like (see the summaries by Weick, 1968; and Lindzey and Byrne, 1968).

IMPOSED STRUCTURES

A number of social institutions and their subgroups have structures formally imposed by authority or custom. The structure formed by lines of authority in military establishments is both widely known and clearly defined. Official tables of organization are even available to indicate clearly the power or authority relations in military groups both large and small. Similarly, flow charts clearly delimiting the system of power relations exist in many industrial organizations. (The term *organization* is customarily used in place of structure for large groups or institutions.) Of course, power or dominance is not the only kind of structure imposed in existing organizations. Communication, work flow, and a number of other relations are common, although some relations are derivative in that they are unintentionally fostered by the official organization charts. Structures that emerge within a group already possessing a formal structure are sometimes called *operating structures.* Operating structures may indeed be partly a function of the formal structure, but they are also a response to the actual demands of the task, people, and setting in which the performance-supporting interaction takes place. When the formal structure is insufficient (out of date, unrealistic, or inefficient), operating structures are especially likely to develop, and the discovery of the operating structure is crucial in understanding the group's performance. Because of etiquette or social pressure, the uncovering of the operating structure is sometimes a delicate and difficult task for the researcher, especially in field research with existing groups.

From the preceding discussions, the nature of the structure concept should be clear. The important question, of course, is whether or not the mere patterning of some particular relation in fact exerts a significant influence on group performance and the social reactions of members, including the way in which an operating structure may develop. If so, is the structure-performance relationship an orderly one, and how may its existence be established? It turns out that such questions are not simple, and even now attempts to summarize such relationships as structure-performance or structure-morale have not been accomplished in a completely satisfactory way. Some of the reasons for this dissatisfaction are theoretical, but before the past couple of decades the major impediments were methodological.

The experimental manipulation of structure, either in the laboratory or in the field, is ordinarily constrained by custom, ethics, or the simple inability of the investigator to impose a genuinely effective structure. It is not possible to make most relations strong enough or make them "take" during the short time the typical laboratory group is in session. Consequently, the kinds of structures that have been investigated by experimental means are surprisingly limited. One relation that has been successfully manipulated as an independent variable, and one which we will consider by way of illustration, is communication.

Communication Networks

Originally stemming from the thinking of Bavelas (1948, 1950), the idea of restricting the persons in a small group so that each member could potentially communicate with some members but not others, led to the notion of a *communication network*. Perhaps because of the formal theoretical tone of the original work (Bavelas, 1948), many workers have been keenly disappointed that research on communication networks has not led to a strong theory of group structure (see the remarks by Glanzer and Glaser, 1961). However, the notion of a communication network is more of a methodological advance than a theoretical innovation. Imposing a communication network upon a small group simply represents one means of manipulating one kind of structure. Other techniques dealing with other structures have been less successful and less thoroughly studied. We will discuss here only the experimental study of communication networks as a basic example of imposed structure.

The simplest question we might ask is whether or not structure (communication structure) makes any difference at all in a group's performance of some task. An important study by Leavitt (1951) attempted to answer this fundamental question with regard to (a) group performance, (b) social process, and (c) personal reactions such as morale. (It is worth noting

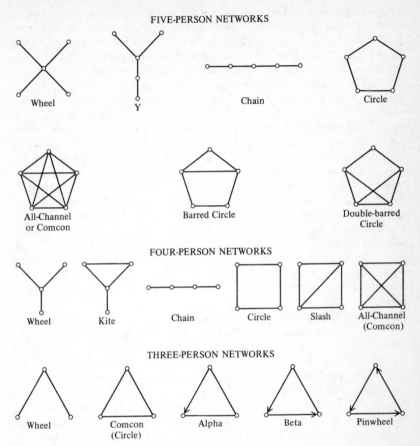

Fig. 5.4 A sample of frequently studied communication networks.

in passing that group research has all too often passed up the opportunity to gather information on *product, social process,* and *personal reactions* within the same experiment). Leavitt required five persons, seated about a table and separated by partitions that prevented face-to-face contact, to communicate only by means of written messages. The centerpost to which the partitions were connected contained a system of slots that was manipulated by the experimenter to yield various networks. The structures investigated by Leavitt are given in the first row of Fig. 5.4: Wheel, Y, Chain, and Circle. The subjects were not aware of the network in which they were placed.

Each group member received a set of cards bearing symbols (asterisk, square, etc.). The group's task was to discover the symbol possessed in common by all members and inform the experimenter as soon as possible.

Each such problem and its solution constituted a trial, and groups were run for several trials. In order to accomplish this simple task, information from all positions must at some point be present at one position in the network; the occupant of that position must then select the common symbol and pass this new information along to the others in order to finish the trial.

Several measures of performance on this "common-symbol problem" were recorded (time, number of errors, number of messages to achieve solution, etc.). Although there were some inconsistencies on any one measure, it was generally concluded that Wheel, Y, Chain, and Circle constituted an order of decreasing performance. If we consider operating patterns, we find that the Wheel, Y, and Chain tended to channel informa- tion to the centermost position, and then symbol-selection messages, indi- cating the symbol to be selected as common, went back to the periphery. This operating structure was fastest for the Wheel and slowest for the Chain. But in all three cases the operating structure that finally developed was stable when once achieved. In general, the Circle had the greatest difficulty in achieving a stable operating structure, and tended to send more messages than other networks; many of these messages were suggestions as to how organization for work might be improved. The members of other networks were more successful than Circle members in deducing the communication pattern in which they were linked.

In addition, persons holding relatively "central" positions tended to evolve as decision makers and were generally judged to be leaders by the other group members. Moreover, persons in central positions, as compared to those in peripheral positions, tended to send more messages, to solve more quickly, to make fewer errors, and to contain persons better satisfied with group and personal efforts.

In other words, the *a priori* "centralness" of the network structure influenced not only group performance, but social process and personal reaction in a fairly orderly way. The results of the Leavitt study are in general accord with related research reported by Bavelas (1950) and Bavelas and Barrett (1951).

Structural indices. The most important outcome of the Leavitt-Bavelas findings is the simple but powerful demonstration that an *a priori* structure produces clear changes in a number of variables associated with group and individual behavior. That is to say, *structure alone* can indeed affect both performance and process in an orderly way. How might these structural features be conveniently summarized? Bavelas introduced the notion of *distance* between two positions, and defined this to be the minimum number of links between the two positions. In order to compare positions within a network, Bavelas suggested the notion of *relative centrality* of a position. The "sum of distances" for a position $(d_{x,y})$ is the sum of the distances from that position to every other position in the network; the sum of these sums of distances may then be taken over every position in the network, giving $\Sigma d_{x,y}$. Finally a position's relative centrality is given by $\Sigma d_{x,y}/d_{x,y}$. The total relative centrality of a network may be obtained by adding the position centralities together.

Relative centrality of positions correlates rather well with performance and personal-reaction measures of positions, but *network centrality* has not been as predictive of group-level variables such as performance. Various remedies have been suggested. Leavitt (1951) proposed a peripherality index (the difference between a position's relative centrality and that of the most central position of the particular network). Shaw (1964) has suggested an independence index; this formulation takes into account for a particular position the number of available channels, the total number of channels in a network, and the number of positions for whch the position in question serves as a *relay.*

We will not consider further the various structure-summarization indices that have been proposed (see Luce, Macy, and Hay, 1954; Flament, 1963; Glanzer and Glaser, 1959; Shaw, 1964), but it is important to realize that no single index has served to summarize structural features in an equally satisfactory way for all the dependent variables that structure apparently influences. In general, the three indices mentioned above have been valuable to some degree for relating structure to position-bound processes, but less satisfactory for helping to explain the differences in performance among the various network types (Shaw, 1964).

Selected Variables and Network Performance

Group size. Earlier conclusions (see Chapter 4) regarding group size and performance are perhaps even more apropos when group structure is involved. While increasing size increases group resources in an obvious way, there is a somewhat less obvious effect on the number of *possible* group structures. If we allow isolates (persons in communication with no one else), permit the development of both one-way and two-way channels, and keep track of particular positions, a five-person group can generate 1,048,576 different structures, but the potential for a three-person group is only 64 structures. Of course, these structures include mirror images and rotations; hence, a large number of the possible structures are trivially different from each other, for it is ordinarily not possible to keep track of functionally identical positions in a way that makes psychological sense. However, consider the simple three-person network in which all channels are two-way and isolates are not considered. In this case, it is not possible to distinguish a Circle from an All-Channel network, and a Chain and Wheel are the same. However, such distinctions were easily drawn for the five-person group. Clearly, there is some difficulty in comparing network type across groups of different size, and this difficulty is not entirely due to differences in member resources.

Despite these comparison difficulties, Shaw (1964) has ventured the conclusion that group size *does not interact* with network type. However, this conclusion must be regarded as highly tentative, not only because of the contingencies between size, possible group structures, and resources, but also because of the as yet poorly understood effects of size on the development of operating structures.

Task type. The early experiments (Bavelas, 1950; Leavitt, 1951) used tasks that were problems only because the subjects were not face-to-face. The "common-symbol problem," described earlier, is a problem principally because group members are not in face-to-face contact. Observe that solution is either impossible for a single subject, through insufficient information, or it is trivially easy through possession of all information (solution). We discussed problems of task taxonomy earlier, and concluded that a general task classification system is not currently available.

However, within the context of the typical network problem, we might make a crude distinction between the *simple* information-diffusion type of task (common-symbol problem) and more *complex* tasks such as arithmetic, sentence construction, and discussion problems of various sorts. If we consider just network performance, it turns out that the simple-complex dichotomy is related to network type in a rather interesting way. The most systematic summary of the relevant evidence is due to Shaw (1964). He has concluded that, in general, the more centralized networks (e.g., Wheel) are faster with *simple* tasks, but the more diffuse networks (e.g., Circle) appear to be superior on *complex* tasks. Roughly the same findings obtain for error rates, although the findings here are less consistent. Although decentralized networks tend to be more active in sending messages than centralized ones, it is difficult to see how this fact alone could account for the performance differences between the centralized and the diffuse networks—especially since a consistent operational organization less often emerges in the diffuse networks during the short time periods employed for most studies.

To explain the centrality-dependent reversal in performance with simple and complex tasks, Shaw (1964) introduces the notions of *independence* and *saturation*. Independence is rather like the freedom of action with which a person may function in his group. Persons in highly central positions have substantial freedom in choosing persons with whom they may communicate, as well as a relatively free hand at collating information and directing more peripheral members. Persons in peripheral positions, by definition, are limited in their communication opportunities and thus less able to facilitate group performance through interaction. Shaw also suggests that the influence of independence is due less to outright organizational influences than to an individual's willingness to perform under the more nearly autonomous conditions. Less independence may limit action possibilities, but it also limits one's motivation to perform. It is not surprising, therefore, that the independence variable may be more closely related to member satisfaction than to performance *per se.*

Saturation, the second major process suggested by Shaw, is essentially the work load accruing to a position either by virtue of the number of channels reporting to it, or by virtue of the information-processing requirements of the task at hand. Thus a high-centrality position in a network is likely to become overloaded more easily when the network faces a complex task than when the task minimizes the information-processing and evaluation requirements accruing to the position.

Shaw has summarized independence and saturation effects as follows (1964, p. 128):

> . . . independence is greater in the decentralized than in the centralized network, regardless of the kind of task. Saturation should be less in the centralized than in the decentralized network with simple tasks, but greater in the centralized network with complex tasks. Therefore, member satisfaction should be greater in more centralized positions, but overall satisfaction should be higher in decentralized networks. With simple tasks, the centralized should be more effective than the decentralized networks; whereas with complex tasks, the decentralized should be more efficient than the centralized networks.

Independence and saturation explain much about network performance and the social behavior of the members. A somewhat related but more parsimonious explanation for the centrality-complexity relationship has to do with distraction. If a problem (e.g., a eureka puzzle or arithmetic problem) does not *require* a division of labor but may be profitably attacked by one person, communication may yield more distraction than aid. Decentralized nets, by definition, contain many positions in which communication demands are low. Such positions, relative to central ones, would enable the occupant to work in a context more closely resembling that of the isolated individual, though perhaps also to benefit from occasional "checking" by others. It was evident in previous chapters that on such problems isolated individuals very often work more efficiently per unit of time than do groups. Of course, this proposal, focusing as it does on the efficiency of the match between task demands, resources, and context, lacks the additional advantages possessed by the saturation-independence hypothesis that deals more easily with process and personal variables.

Communication mode. It is well known that persons send and receive information in a very large variety of ways. You may recall many social gatherings at which the content of your remarks was less important than the manner of their delivery. Most persons feel that they are sensitive to a wide variety of facial cues, gestures, and the like, as well as to the intonations and inflections accompanying an utterance. As indicated by our earlier discussion of eye contact, much research attests to the importance of non-verbal as well as verbal cues in interaction. Indeed, the very complexity of the social exchange process has been suggested earlier as one impediment to effective research on interaction phenomena.

Gradually, techniques for appropriate experimental research have emerged; the notion of a communication network has been one such important device. Clearly, the separation of group members rules out, and thus controls, many of the important nonverbal cues. To be sure, a number of groups organized for effective performance do in fact exchange information or interact at a distance (as it were), and the network is perhaps a crude laboratory analog for such situations. Communication by memoranda, letters, and the like is indeed a common feature of many groups whose members are divided by time or distance. Communication by intercom and telephone, however, is also common in many groups whose members are not in a face-to-face relation.

In principal, the network idea should be applicable to direct vocal exchange; the term "radio net" has, in fact, been used in a somewhat similar way by the military services for many years. It is therefore quite surprising that so little attention has been devoted to the experimental study of networks in which members communicate by intercom. Only two such studies appear to be available (Heise and Miller, 1951; Davis and Hornseth, 1967). [Lanzetta and Roby (1956) have reported studies in which visually isolated group members communicated by intercom, but these groups did not constitute networks in the sense of physically patterned communication channels.]

Heise and Miller (1951) required three-person groups to work on three different kinds of tasks (word construction, sentence construction, and anagrams) in five different networks. The network types are given the bottom row of Fig. 5.4. Heise and Miller also introduced noise to the intercom system in such a way that the signal-to-noise ratio varied over three ranges of intelligibility. They found that the Comcon was most efficient for word-construction problems, with the "completely directional" (Pinwheel) network (shown as the last net in the three-person row of Fig. 5.4) the least efficient. The sentence-construction problem yielded essentially the same results, except that the Comcon was second to the Wheel. No significant ordering of networks appeared for the anagram problem. Increasing the noise level seemed to accentuate the differences among networks for the first two problems, but was not effective for the anagram problems; in the latter problems the performance discrepancy among the various nets was negligible.

The discrepancy in results between the anagram problems and the other tasks is a most interesting one. The solution of anagrams (rearranging scrambled letters to form a word) does not depend on any experimenter-produced information, whereas information for the other two problems was divided and assigned by the experimenter to the members in a manner similar to the common-symbol problem we encountered in the message-passing networks. The anagram problem is thus an abstract problem that does not necessarily benefit from a division of labor or information exchange among the members of a group prior to agreement upon a solution. In our earlier discussion of group performance we pointed out the importance of the match between the task requirements and the social process necessary or sufficient for performing the task. Hence, Heise and Miller's experiment provides no evidence that the particular communication pattern exerts a strong influence when the task is an abstract problem that is at the same time independent of interaction.

Unfortunately, Heise and Miller did not collect much interaction or person-reaction data. Moreover, only three subjects were used in the word-construction and sentence-construction conditions, and only two groups of three persons were available for the anagram condition. These procedural nuances and confounds have seriously hampered the usefulness of Heise and Miller's results.

In a more recent experiment, Davis and Hornseth (1967) used five-person Wheel, Circle, and "completely connected" (Comcon) networks in which an intercom system was used to manipulate the communication channels. The tasks were eureka problems similar in many ways to anagrams: a word puzzle and a modified water-jar problem similar to the one described earlier. Both problems were also solved independently by a sample of individual subjects. In addition to performance data, Davis and Hornseth tabulated interaction rate and recorded personal reactions following work on the tasks.

As in Heise and Miller's results, the relative difference in performance among networks was not large. However, the Comcon network was both faster in achieving an answer and higher in number of correct solutions than the other two networks. Wheels and Circles did not consistently differ on speed or rate of correct solutions. Perhaps the most interesting comparisons were those between the Comcon network and (a) the individual subjects who worked alone and (b) the theoretical predictions from the Lorge and Solomon Model A. (Recall that Model A sets a stringent baseline, in that it assumes that the best solution among members is recognized and produced by the group as soon as it occurs.) For both problems, the Comcon was the network performing, on the average, most clearly in excess of the individual subjects, and at the same time most nearly in accord with the Lorge-Solomon baseline.

The personal reactions of members (such as morale) were not so clearly defined as in the message-passing networks, but were generally consistent with the personal reactions in these networks—the Circle fostered greater satisfaction than Wheel, with the Comcon falling between these two extremes. Large and orderly differences in amount of discussions were evident among networks—Comcon talked the most and Wheel the least. Apparently action followed opportunity.

What might account for the finding that *minimal a priori organization* (Comcon) apparently provided the closest approach to efficient performance for networks whose members communicated "directly"? Davis and Hornseth answer that question as follows (1967, pp. 101-102):

> One explanation is that, given the random assignment of subjects, Comcon is more flexible than any other pattern could possibly be—a larger number of "operational" patterns or communication sequences are logically possible. In any organization with restrictions, say the Wheel, the position of high centrality may be filled by a person of modest intelligence or restrained enthusiasm. Such a person can function profitably in the simple business of recognizing symbols and passing messages, for anything which moves the mass along is helpful. But an intellectually challenging problem may require communication of a more sophisticated nature. Thoughtful reflection, evaluation of a possible solution, and the like may require more ability than that possessed by the man filling the high-centrality position. The Comcon, unlike the Wheel, can develop the talents which have fallen to its lot, by giving some members a more important role to play, or at least by going around any person who is blocking work. Circle nets are also limited in the degree of circumvention possible. Thus, the degree to which alternative structures can emerge is minimal in a Wheel and maximal in a Comcon network. Prior to group activity member abilities are not known. Comcon, at least, permits some utilization of abilities discovered during work.

Observe that the above explanation is not dissimilar to the notion of *saturation* proposed by Shaw (1964). A number of other findings indeed tended to support the major performance findings, but we shall not explore them further. Suffice it to say that the combination of vocal communication mode and abstract problems that are meaningful tasks for the isolated individual apparently produces a rather different situation than do the message-passing and information-dispersion problems discussed earlier. In particular, the ease with which direct communication proceeds may attenuate the network variable in such a way that its influence is a subtle one, requiring perhaps more sensitive measurement settings than those provided by either the Heise-Miller or the Davis-Hornseth experiments—if, in fact, communication pattern is actually as important to talking groups as it is to message-passing groups.

Communication Networks: Concluding Remarks

A number of other important relationships between imposed communication structures and performance have been observed, but we are unable to explore them at length here. The simple finding that communication structure *is* related to a number of group output variables constitutes, of course, the major conclusion. That this relationship stems from the actual experience of persons interacting in a structured setting, and not merely from physical limitations alone, is well illustrated by studies in which the group begins work in one network pattern but later changes to another network possessing different properties (Lawson, 1961; Cohen and Bennis, 1961; Cohen, 1961, 1962). Groups developing an efficient operating structure (such as typically arises in a Wheel) continue that efficient system in the second network, provided the second net permits them to do so. Thus Wheel-to-Circle is a more viable progression than Circle-to-Wheel or Circle-to-Circle.

However, as was mentioned earlier, the findings from the communication network studies, which constitute our most precise means of investigating the effects of structure to date, are not as orderly as it was originally hoped they would be. Some writers feel that after nearly two decades of research the inconsistencies in the findings are embarrassingly prominent (Burgess, 1968a, 1968b). There are two important observations, however, that do much to place communication networks in perspective.

First, the imposition of communication restrictions and regulation of communication flow is a *technique,* not a close analog of particular groups or organizations. As a technique for experimentation, the chief importance of the communication network lies more in its potential as a tool for basic investigation than in the immediate production of findings applicable to existing groups that have a *prima facie* similarity to a Wheel, a "Y," or the like. In addition, it should come as no surprise that communication restriction plays an important role in group performance, but is susceptible to interaction with other personal and social variables long known to affect the behavior of groups.

Second, in the past there has been insufficient attention devoted to the question of *how* and *why* the imposition of a communication network yields its effects. Clearly, "something happens" differently in different networks, and group performance is frequently influenced in a strong way. Centrality, saturation, independence, and other concepts aid in ordering these phenomena, but they do not constitute a viable theory. The key to the development of an orderly understanding may stem from emphasizing the role of a network's *operating structure,* a notion introduced earlier. The importance of an operating structure was carefully described several years ago by Guetzkow and Simon (1955), but has generally been ignored. Guetzkow and Simon pointed out that, given the opportunity to develop maximally efficient operating structures, ". . . there is no difference in the limiting times for task performance between groups in the unrestricted net (the All-Channel groups) and those in the restricted nets (the Wheel and Circle groups)" (1955, p. 239).

Perhaps even more striking support for the importance of operating structures comes from Leavitt and Knight (1963). They demonstrate (at least for the message-passing nets working on information-dispersion problems), on logical grounds alone, that some operating structures rarely or never used by subjects can turn even the Circle into an efficient problem-solving network. Circles operating as "Chains" are generally believed to be most efficient, but Leavitt and Knight show that there exists another Circle-as-Circle operation that yields a most efficient solution. It is easy to become bogged down in details at this point, but it is precisely such inattention to details, sometimes quite obvious in retrospect, that has flawed the development of explanations of network effects on group performance and process. (Leavitt and Knight even suggest that the historical accident that the original studies used odd-numbered rather than even-numbered groups obscured the point they are making!)

In any event, the emergence of an operating structure within the imposed communication structure requires both time and opportunity. A recent series of studies by Burgess (1968b) documents the assertion that, after being in existence for some time, quite different extremes (Wheel and Circle) develop "steady states" (efficient operating structures) that are reflected in negligible differences in performance between the two networks. In the early phases of their existence (the first 50 problems or so), the typical differences between networks were observed; but after a steady state was reached (900 to 1100 problems), the Wheel and Circle performed in a similar way. These findings are, of course, quite consistent with Guetzkow and Simon's conclusions.

The preceding remarks should not be interpreted as suggesting that our knowledge about imposed structures, derived from the study of communication networks, is either trivial or artifactual. On the contrary, the important lesson to be drawn is that the richness of the group-structure concept and the complexity of the ways in which it can interact with other variables have only recently begun to receive full appreciation—even after nearly two decades of intensive empirical effort.

Finally, we might observe that the important goal in the years ahead is to bring *other relations*—that is, structures differentiated on other variables, such as dominance, affection, etc.—under the same sort of experimental control that has been developed for communication. These other interpersonal relations, however, often involve important ethical and practical problems. Only occasionally have researchers attempted to manipulate important interpersonal relations among more than two persons at one time.

References

Abel, T. M., The influence of social facilitation on motor performance at different levels of intelligence. *American Journal of Psychology*, 1938, **51**, 379-389.

Ader, R., and R. Tatum, Free-operant avoidance conditioning in individual and paired human subjects. *Journal of Experimental Animal Behavior*, 1963, **6**, 357-359.

Allport, F. H., *Social psychology*. Boston: Houghton Mifflin, 1924.

Anderson, C. A., An experimental study of "social facilitation" as affected by intelligence. *American Journal of Sociology*, 1929, **34**, 874-881.

Anderson, N. H., Group performance in an anagram task. *Journal of Social Psychology*, 1961, **55**, 67-75.

Argyle, M., *The psychology of interpersonal behavior*, Baltimore: Penguin, 1967.

Back, K. W., Influence through social communication. *Journal of Abnormal Social Psychology*, 1951, **46**, 9-23.

Bales, R. F., F. L. Strodtbeck, T. M. Mills, and Mary E. Roseborough, Channels of communication in small groups. *American Sociological Review*, 1951, **16**, 461-468.

Bandura, A., Vicarious processes: a case of no-trial learning. In L. Berkowitz (Ed.), *Advances in experimental social psychology*. Vol. 2. New York: Academic Press, 1965a. Pp. 1-55.

Bandura, A., Influence of models' reinforcement contingencies on the acquisition of imitative responses. *Journal of Personality and Social Psychology*, 1965b, **1**, 589-595.

Bandura, W., and R. Walters, *Social learning and personality development*. New York: Holt, Rinehart and Winston, 1963.

Bavelas, A., A mathematical model for group structure. *Applied Anthropology*, 1948, **7**, 16-30.

Bavelas, A., Communication patterns in task-oriented groups. *Journal of the Acoustical Society of America*, 1950, **22**, 725-730.

Bavelas, A., and D. Barrett, An experimental approach to organizational communication. *Personnel*, 1951, **27**, 367-371.

Bayer, E., Beiträge zur Zweikomponententheorie des Hungers. *Zeitschrift für Psychologie*, 1929, **112**, 1-54. [Cited in R. B. Zajonc, Social facilitation. *Science*, 1965, **149**, 269-274.]

Berkowitz, L., Group standards, cohesiveness, and productivity. *Human Relations*, 1954, **7**, 505-519.

Berkowitz, L., *Aggression: a social psychological analysis*. New York: McGraw-Hill, 1962.

Berkowitz, L., The effects of observing violence. *Scientific American*, 1964, **210**, 35-42.

Berkowitz, L., Some aspects of observed aggression. *Journal of Personality and Social Psychology*, 1965, **2**, 359-369.

Berkowitz, L., and R. G. Geen, Film violence and the cue properties of available targets. *Journal of Personality and Social Psychology*, 1966, **3**, 525-530.

Berkowitz, L., and E. Rawlings, Effects of film violence on inhibitions against subsequent aggression. *Journal of Abnormal Social Psychology*, 1963, **66**, 405-412.

Borgatta, E. F., A diagnostic note on the construction of sociograms and action diagrams. *Group Psychotherapy*, 1951, **3**, 300-308.

Bourne, L. E., Jr., and W. F. Battig, Complex processes. In J. B. Sidowski (Ed.), *Experimental methods and instrumentation in psychology*. New York: McGraw-Hill, 1966. Pp. 541-576.

Brown, R., *Social psychology*. New York: The Free Press, 1965.

Burgess, R. L., Communication networks: an experimental reevaluation. *Journal of Experimental Social Psychology*, 1968a, **4**, 324-337.

Burgess, R. L., An experimental and mathematical analysis of group behavior within restricted networks. *Journal of Experimental Social Psychology*, 1968b, **4**, 338-349.

Burton, A., The influence of social factors upon the persistence of satiation in pre-school children. *Child Development*, 1941, **12**, 121-129.

Cartwright, D., and A. Zander, *Group dynamics: research and theory*. New York: Harper and Row, 1968.

Chen, S. C., Social modification of the activity of ants in nest-building. *Physiological Zoology*, 1937, **10**, 420-436.

Cohen, A. M., Changing small-group communication networks. *Journal of Communication*, 1961, **11**, 116-124.

Cohen, A. M., Changing small-group communication networks. *Administrative Quarterly,* 1962, **6**, 443-462.

Cohen, A. M., and W. G. Bennis, Continuity of leadership in communication networks. *Human Relations,* 1961, **14**, 351-368.

Collins, B. E., and H. Guetzkow, *A social psychology of group processes for decision making.* New York: Wiley, 1964.

Cottrell, N. B., Performance in the presence of other human beings: mere presence, audience, and affiliation effects. In E. C. Simmel, R. A. Hoppe, and G. A. Milton (Eds.), *Social facilitation and imitative behavior.* Boston, Mass.: Allyn and Bacon, 1968.

Darley, J. M., and B. Latané, Bystander intervention in emergencies: diffusion of responsibility. *Journal of Personality and Social Psychology,* 1968, **8**, 377-383.

Dashiell, J. F., An experimental analysis of some group effects. *Journal of Abnormal and Social Psychology,* 1930, **25**, 190-199.

Dashiell, J. F., Experimental studies of the influence of social situations on the behavior of individual human adults. In C. Murchison (Ed.), *A handbook of social psychology.* Worcester, Mass.: Clark University Press, 1935. Pp. 1097-1158.

Davis, J. H., Models for the classification of problems and the prediction of group problem-solving from individual results. Unpublished doctoral dissertation, Michigan State University, 1961.

Davis, J. H., The preliminary analysis of emergent group structure. *Psychometrika,* 1963, **28**, 189-198.

Davis, J. H., Individual and group problem solving, subject preference, and task type. *Journal of Personality and Social Psychology,* 1969, in press.

Davis, J. H., M. H. Carey, P. N. Foxman, and D. R. Tarr, Verbalization, experimenter presence, and problem solving. *Journal of Personality and Social Psychology,* 1968, **8**, 299-302.

Davis, J. H., R. A. Hoppe, and J. P. Hornseth, Risk-taking: task, response pattern, and grouping. *Organizational Behavior and Human Performance,* 1968, **3**, 124-142.

Davis, J. H., and J. Hornseth, Discussion patterns and word problems. *Sociometry,* 1967, **30**, 91-103.

Davis, J. H., and F. Restle, The analysis of problems and prediction of group problem solving. *Journal of Abnormal and Social Psychology,* 1963, **66**, 103-116.

Deutsch, M., An experimental study of the effects of cooperation and competition upon group process. *Human Relations,* 1949, **2**, 199-231.

Deutsch, M., The effects of cooperation and competition upon group process. In D. Cartwright and A. Zander, *Group Dynamics.* New York: Harper and Row, 1968. Pp. 461-482.

Dunnette, M. D., J. Campbell, and K. Jaastad, The effect of group participation on brain storming effectiveness for two industrial samples. *Journal of Applied Psychology*, 1963, **47**, 30-37.

Faust, W. L., Group versus individual problem-solving. *Journal of Abnormal and Social Psychology*, 1959, **59**, 68-72.

Feofanov, M. P., K voprosu ob izuchenii strukturnykh osobennostei kollektivov. [The question of investigating the structural characteristics of a group.] *Zh. psikhol. pedol. i psikhotekh.*, 1928, **1**, 107-120. P. A. 3: 4117 [Cited in A. P. Hare, *Handbook of small group research*. New York: Free Press of Glencoe, 1962. P. 346.]

Festinger, L., H. W. Riecken, Jr., and S. Schachter, *When prophecy fails*. Minneapolis: University of Minnesota Press, 1956.

Flament, C., Applications of graph theory to group structure. Englewood Cliffs, N.J.: Prentice-Hall, 1963.

Flanders, J. P., and D. L. Thistlethwaite, Effects of familiarization and group discussion upon risk taking. *Journal of Personality and Social Psychology*, 1967, **5**, 91-97.

French, J. R. P., Jr., The disruption and cohesion of groups. *Journal of Abnormal and Social Psychology*, 1941, **36**, 361-377.

Gates, G. S., The effect of an audience upon performance. *Journal of Abnormal and Social Psychology*, 1924, **18**, 334-342.

Gergen, K. J., *The psychology of behavior exchange*. Reading, Mass.: Addison-Wesley, 1969.

Gibb, J. R., The effects of group size and of threat reduction upon creativity in a problem-solving situation. *American Psychologist*, 1951, **6**, 324.

Glanzer, M., and R. Glaser, Techniques for the study of group structure and behavior: I. Analysis of structure. *Psychological Bulletin*, 1959, **56**, 317-332.

Glanzer, M., and R. Glaser, Techniques for the study of group structure and behavior: II. Empirical studies of the effects of structure in small groups. *Psychological Bulletin*, 1961, **58**, 1-27.

Gordon, K., A Study of esthetic judgments. *Journal of Experimental Psychology*, 1923, **6**, 36-43.

Guetzkow, H., and H. A. Simon, The impact of certain communication nets upon organization and performance in task-oriented groups. *Management Science*, 1955, **1**, 233-250.

Gurnee, H., Maze learning in the collective situation. *Journal of Psychology*, 1937, **3**, 437-443.

Gurnee, H., The effect of collective learning upon the individual participants. *Journal of Abnormal and Social Psychology*, 1939, **34**, 529-532.

Gurnee, H., Learning under competitive and collaborative sets. *Journal of Experimental Social Psychology*, 1968, **4**, 26-34.

Harary, F., R. Z. Norman, and Z. Cartwright, *Structural models: an introduction to the theory of directed graphs.* New York: Wiley, 1965.

Hare, A. P., *Handbook of small group research.* New York: Free Press, 1962.

Harlow, H. F., Social facilitation of feeding in the albino rat. *Journal of Genetic Psychology,* 1932, **43**, 211-221.

Harlow, H. F., and M. K. Harlow, The affectional systems. In A. M. Schrier, H. F. Harlow, and F. Stollnitz (Eds.), *Behavior of nonhuman primates.* Vol. II. New York: Academic Press, 1965. Pp. 287-334.

Heise, G. A., and G. A. Miller, Problem solving by small groups using various communication nets. *Journal of Abnormal and Social Psychology,* 1951, **46**, 327-335.

Henchy, T., and D. C. Glass, Evaluation apprehension and the social facilitation of dominant and subordinate responses. *Journal of Personality and Social Psychology,* 1968, **4**, 446-454.

Heslin, R., Predicting group task effectiveness from member characteristics. *Psychological Bulletin,* 1964, **62**, 248-256.

Hoppe, R. A., Memorizing by individuals and groups: a test of the pooling-of-ability model. *Journal of Abnormal and Social Psychology,* 1962, **65**, 64-67.

Husband, R. W., Cooperative versus solitary problem solution. *Journal of Social Psychology,* 1940, **11**, 405-409.

Ichheiser, G., Über die Veränderung der Leistungsbereitschaft durch das Bewusstsein einen Zuschauer zu haben. [Changes in performance through consciousness of a spectator.] *Psychotechnische Zeitschrift,* 1930, **5**, 52-53. [Cited by G. Murphy and L. B. Murphy, *Experimental social psychology.* New York: Harper, 1931.]

Jackson, J., Structural characteristics of norms. In Ivan D. Steiner and Martin Fishbein (Eds.), *Current studies in social psychology.* New York: Holt, Rinehart and Winston, 1965.

Jennings, H. H., *Leadership and isolation* (2nd ed.) New York: Longmans, Green, 1950.

Johnson, D. M., *The psychology of thought and judgment.* New York: Harper, 1955.

Johnson, H. H., and J. M. Torcivia, Group and individual performance on a single-stage task as a function of distribution of individual performance. *Journal of Experimental Social Psychology,* 1967, **3**, 266-273.

Kelley, H. H., Interpersonal accommodation. *American Psychologist,* 1968, **23**, 399-410.

Kelley, H. H., and J. W. Thibaut, Experimental studies of group problem solving and process. In G. Lindzey (Ed.), *Handbook of social psychology.* Vol. II. Reading, Mass.: Addison-Wesley, 1954. Pp. 735-785.

Kiesler, C. A., and Sara B. Kiesler, *Conformity.* Reading, Mass.: Addison-Wesley, 1969.

Knight, H. C., A comparison of the reliability of group and individual judgments. Master's essay in Columbia University Library, 1921. [Cited in G. Murphy and L. B. Murphy, *Experimental social psychology.* New York: Harper, 1931.]

Kogan, N., and M. A. Wallach, Risk taking as a function of the situation, the person, and the group. In *New directions in psychology III.* New York: Holt, Rinehart and Winston, 1967. Pp. 111-278.

Krech, D., R. S. Crutchfield, and E. L. Ballachey, *Individual in society.* New York: McGraw-Hill, 1962.

Laird, D. A., Changes in motor control and individual variations under the influence of "razzing." *Journal of Experimental Psychology,* 1923, **6**, 236-246.

Lanzetta, J. T., and T. B. Roby, Effects of work group structure and certain variables on group performance. *Journal of Abnormal and Social Psychology,* 1956, **53**, 307-314.

Latané, B., and A. J. Arrowood, Monitoring of test equipment. *Journal of Applied Psychology,* 1963, **47**, 324-327.

Laughlin, P. R., Selection strategies in concept attainment as a function of number of persons and stimulus display. *Journal of Experimental Psychology,* 1965, **5**, 115-119.

Laughlin, P. R. and M. A. Doherty, Discussion versus memory in cooperative group concept attainment. *Journal of Educational Psychology,* 1967, **58**, 123-128.

Laughlin, P. R., and R. P. McGlynn, Cooperative versus competitive concept attainment as a function of sex and stimulus display. *Journal of Personality and Social Psychology,* in press.

Laughlin, P. R., P. R. McGlynn, J. A. Anderson, and E. S. Jacobson, Concept attainment by individuals versus cooperative pairs as a function of memory, sex, and concept rule. *Journal of Personality and Social Psychology,* 1968, 8, 410-417.

Lawson, E. D., Change in communication nets and performance. Paper read at the Eastern Psychological Association Convention, 1961.

Leavitt, H. J., Some effects of certain patterns on group performance. *Journal of Abnormal and Social Psychology,* 1951, **46**, 38-50.

Leavitt, H. J. and K. E. Knight, Most "efficient" solutions to communication networks: empirical versus analytical search. *Sociometry,* 1963, **26**, 260-267.

Le Bon, G., *Psychologie des foules.* Paris: F. Olean, 1895. Translation, *The crowd.* London: T. Fisher Unwin, 1896.

Leuba, C. J., An experimental study of rivalry in young children. *Journal of Comparative Psychology,* 1933, **16**, 367-378.

Lichtenstein, S., P. Slovic, and D. Zink, Effect of instruction in expected value upon optimality of gambling decisions. *Oregon Research Institute Research Bulletin,* Vol. 8, No. 1, March 1968.

Lindzey, G., and D. Byrne, Measurement of social choice and interpersonal attractiveness. In G. Lindzey and E. Aronson (Eds.), *The handbook of social psychology*. Vol. II. Reading, Mass.: Addison-Wesley, 1968. Pp. 452-525.

Lonergan, B. G., and C. G. McClintock, Effects of group membership on risk-taking behavior. *Psychological Reports*, 1961, **8**, 447-455.

Lorge, I., D. Fox, J. Davitz, and M. Brenner, A survey of studies contrasting the quality of group performance and individual performance, 1920-1957. *Psychological Bulletin*, 1958, **55**, 337-372.

Lorge, I., and H. Solomon, Two models of group behavior in the solution of eureka-type problems. *Psychometrika*, 1955, **20**, 139-148.

Luce, R. D., J. Macy, and D. H. Hay, Information flow in task-oriented groups. Research Laboratory of Electronics Technical Report No. 264, 1954, Massachusetts Institute of Technology, Cambridge, Mass.

McCurdy, H. G. and W. E. Lambert, The efficiency of small human groups in the solution of problems requiring genuine cooperation. *Journal of Personality*, 1952, **20**, 478-494.

McDougall, W., *Introduction to social psychology*. London: Methuen, 1908.

McGrath, J. E. and J. E. Altman, *Small group research*. New York: Holt, Rinehart and Winston, 1966.

Mann, R. D., A review of the relationships between personality and performance in small groups. *Psychological Bulletin*, 1959, **56**, 241-270.

Marquart, D. I., Group problem solving. *Journal of Social Psychology*, 1955, **41**, 103-113.

Marquis, D. G., Individual responsiblity and group decisions involving risk. *Industrial Management Review*, 1962, **3**, 8-23.

Marquis, D. G., Individual and group decisions involving risk. Working paper, Alfred P. Sloan School of Management, Massachusetts Institute of Technology, March 1968.

Marquis, D. G., H. Guetzkow, and R. W. Heyns, A social psychological study of the decision-making conference. In H. Guetzkow (Ed.), *Groups, leadership, and men: research in human relations*. Pittsburgh: Carnegie Press, 1951. Pp. 55-67.

Mayer, A., Über Einzel und Gesamtleistung des Schulkindes. [On the school child's work alone and in the group.] *Arch. ges. Psychol.*, 1903, **1**, 276-416. [Cited in G. Murphy and L. B. Murphy, *Experimental social psychology*. New York: Harper, 1931.]

Meumann, E., *Haus- und Schularbeit* [*Home and school work*], 1914. [Cited in G. Murphy and L. B. Murphy, *Experimental social psychology*. New York: Harper, 1931.]

Milgram, S., Some conditions of obedience and disobedience to authority. In I. D. Steiner and M. Fishbein (Eds.), *Current studies in social psychology*. New York: Holt, Rinehart and Winston, 1965.

Miller, N. E., and J. Dollard, *Social learning and imitation*. New Haven: Yale University Press, 1941.

Murphy, G., and L. B. Murphy, *Experimental social psychology*. New York: Harper, 1931.

Nordhøy, F., Group interaction in decision-making under risk. Unpublished Master's thesis, Massachusetts Institute of Technology, School of Industrial Management, 1962.

Oeser, O. A., and G. O'Brien, A mathematical model for structural role theory: III. *Human Relations,* 1967, **20**, 83-97.

Olson, P., and J. H. Davis, Divisible tasks and pooling performance in groups. *Psychological Reports,* 1964, **15**, 511-517.

Osborn, A. F., *Applied imagination.* New York: Scribners, 1957.

Parnes, S. J., and A. Meadow, University of Buffalo research regarding development of creative talent. In C. W. Taylor (Ed.), *The third University of Utah research conference on the identification of creative scientific talent.* University of Utah, 1959.

Perlmutter, J. V., and G. de Montmollin, Group learning of nonsense syllables. *Journal of Abnormal and Social Psychology,* 1952, **47**, 762-769.

Pessin, J., The comparative effects of social and mechanical stimulation on memorizing. *American Journal of Psychology,* 1933, **45**, 263-270.

Platt, J. R., Strong inference. *Science,* 1964, **146**, 347-353.

Posner, M. E., Information reduction in the analysis of sequential tasks. *Psychological Review,* 1964, **71**, 491-504.

Proctor, C. H., and C. P. Loomis, Analysis of sociometric data. In Marie Jahoda, M. Deutsch, and S. W. Cook (Eds.), *Research methods in social relations: with especial reference to prejudice.* Part 2. New York: Dryden, 1951.

Raven, B. H., and J. Rietsema, The effects of varied clarity of group goal and group path upon the individual and his relation to his group. *Human Relations,* 1957, **10**, 29-45.

Restle, F., and J. H. Davis, Success and speed of problem solving by individuals and groups. *Psychological Review,* 1962, **69**, 520-536.

Roby, T. B., and J. T. Lanzetta, Considerations in the analysis of group tasks. *Psychological Bulletin,* 1958, **55**, 88-101.

Roethlisberger, F. J., and W. J. Dickson, *Management and the Worker.* Cambridge, Mass.: Harvard University Press, 1939.

Rommetveit, R., *Social norms and roles: explorations in the psychology of enduring social pressures.* Minneapolis: University of Minnesota Press, 1955.

Schachter, S., Deviation, rejection, and communication. *Journal of Abnormal Social Psychology,* 1951, **46**, 190-207.

Schachter, S., *The psychology of affiliation.* Stanford, Calif.: Stanford University Press, 1959.

Schachter, S., N. Ellertson, D. McBride, and D. Gregory, An experimental study of cohesiveness and productivity. *Human Relations,* 1951, **4**, 229-238.

Schelling, T. C., The strategy of conflict: prospectus for a reorientation of game theory. *Journal of Conflict Resolution*, 1958, 2, 203-264.

Schmidt, F., Experimentelle Untersuchungen über die Hausaufgaben des Schulkindes. [Experimental studies of the school child's homework.] *Sammlung von Abhandlungen zur Psychologie und Pädagogie*, 1904, 1, 181-300. [Cited in G. Murphy and L. B. Murphy, *Experimental social psychology*. New York: Harper, 1931.]

Seidman, D., S. B. Bensen, I. Miller, and T. Meeland, Influence of a partner on tolerance for self-administered electric shock. *Journal of Abnormal Social Psychology*, 1957, 54, 210-212.

Sengupta, N. N., and C. P. N. Sinha, Mental work in isolation and in group. *Indian Journal of Psychology*, 1926, 1, 106-110.

Shapiro, D., and P. H. Leiderman, Acts and activation: a psychophysiological study of social interaction. In P. H. Leiderman and D. Shapiro (Eds.), *Psychobiological approaches to social behavior*. Stanford, Calif.: Stanford University Press, 1964. Pp. 110-126.

Shapiro, D., and P. H. Leiderman, Arousal correlates of task role and group setting. *Journal of Personality and Social Psychology*, 1967, 5, 103-107.

Shaw, Marjorie E., Comparison of individuals and small groups in the rational solution of complex problems. *American Journal of Psychology*, 1932, 44, 491-504.

Shaw, M. E., Acceptance of authority, group structure, and the effectiveness of small groups. *Journal of Personality*, 1959, 27, 196-210.

Shaw, M. E., Scaling group tasks: a method for dimensional analysis. Technical Report No. 1, July 1963, Office of Naval Research Contract NR 170-266, Nonr-580 (11).

Shaw, M. E., Communication networks. In L. Berkowitz (Ed.), *Advances in experimental social psychology*. New York: Academic Press, 1964.

Sherif, M., *The psychology of social norms*. New York: Harper, 1936.

Sherif, M., and C. Sherif, *Groups in harmony and tension*. New York: Harper and Row, 1953.

Shevaleva, E., and O. Ergolska, [Children's collectives in the light of experimental reflexology.] Sbornik, posvyzshennyi V. M. Bekhterevu k 40-135nyu professorskow dyatelnosti [Bekhterev 40th anniversary commemorative volume], 1926, 147-182. P. A. 1: 2486. [Cited in A. P. Hare, *Handbook of small group research*. New York: Free Press of Glencoe, 1962. P. 346.

Shubik, M. (Ed.), *Game theory and related approaches to social behavior*. New York: Wiley, 1964.

Smoke, W. H., and R. B. Zajonc, On the reliability of group judgments and decisions. In J. H. Criswell, H. Solomon, and P. Suppes (Eds.), *Mathematical methods in small group processes*. Stanford, Calif.: Stanford University Press, 1962. Pp. 322-333.

Sommer, R., Studies in personal space. *Sociometry*, 1959, 22, 247-260.

Sommer, R., Leadership and group geography. *Sociometry,* 1961, **24,** 99-110.

Sommer, R., The distance for comfortable conversation: a further study. *Sociometry,* 1962, **25,** 111-116.

Steiner, I. D., Models for inferring relationships between group size and potential group productivity. *Behavioral Science,* 1966, **11,** 273-283.

Steiner, I. D. and N. Rajaratnam, A model for the comparison of individual and group performance scores. *Behavioral Science,* 1961, **6,** 142-147.

Stephan, F. F., and E. G. Mishler, The distribution of participation in small groups: an exponential approximation. *American Sociological Review,* 1952, **17,** 203-207.

Stoner, J. A. F., Risky and cautious shifts in group decisions: the influence of widely held values. Working paper, Alfred P. Sloan School of Management, Massachusetts Institute of Technology, October 1967.

Stroop, J. B., Is the judgment of the group better than that of the average member of the group? *Journal of Experimental Psychology,* 1932, **15,** 550-560.

Taylor, D. W., *Problem solving by groups.* Proceedings of the Fourteenth International Congress of Psychology, Montreal, June 1954.

Taylor, D. W., P. C. Berry, and C. H. Block, Does group participation when using brainstorming facilitate or inhibit creative thinking? *Administrative Science Quarterly,* **3,** 1958, 23-47.

Taylor, D. W., and W. L. Faust, Twenty questions: efficiency in problem solving as a function of size of group. *Journal of Experimental Psychology,* 1952, **44,** 360-368.

Taylor, J. H., C. E. Thompson, and D. Spassoff, The effect of conditions of work and various suggested attitudes on production and reported feelings of tiredness and boredness. *Journal of Applied Psychology,* 1937, **21,** 431-450.

Teger, A. I., and D. G. Pruitt, Components of group risk taking. *Journal of Experimental Social Psychology,* 1967, **3,** 189-205.

Thorndike, R. L., On what type of task will a group do well? *Journal of Abnormal and Social Psychology,* 1938, **33,** 409-413.

Travis, L. E., The effect of a small audience upon eye-hand coordination. *Journal of Abnormal and Social Psychology,* 1925, **20,** 142-146.

Triplett, N., The dynamogenic factors in pacemaking competition. *American Journal of Psychology,* 1898, **9,** 507-533.

Wallach, M. A., N. Kogan, and D. J. Bem, Group influence on individual risk taking. *Journal of Abnormal and Social Psychology,* 1962, **65,** 75-86.

Wallach, M. A., N. Kogan, and D. J. Bem, Diffusion of responsibility and level of risk taking in groups. *Journal of Abnormal and Social Psychology,* 1964, **68,** 263-274.

Wallach, M. A., N. Kogan, and R. B. Burt, Are risk takers more persuasive than conservatives in group discussions? *Journal of Experimental Social Psychology,* 1968, **4**, 76-88.

Walters, R. H., and R. D. Parke, Social motivation, dependency, and susceptibility to social influence. In L. Berkowitz (Ed.), *Advances in experimental social psychology.* Vol. I. New York: Academic Press, 1964. Pp. 231-276.

Wapner, S., and T. G. Alper, The effect of an audience on behavior in a choice situation. *Journal of Abnormal Social Psychology,* 1952, **47**, 222-229.

Watson, G. B., Do groups think more efficiently than individuals? *Journal of Abnormal and Social Psychology,* 1928, **23**, 328-336.

Webb, E. J., D. T. Campbell, R. D. Schwartz, and L. Sechrest. *Unobtrusive measures.* Chicago: Rand McNally, 1966.

Weick, K. E., Systematic observational methods. In G. Lindzey and E. Aronson (Eds.), *The handbook of social psychology.* Vol. II. Reading, Mass.: Addison-Wesley, 1968.

Wrightsman, L. S., Jr., Effects of waiting with others on changes in level of felt anxiety. *Journal of Abnormal and Social Psychology,* 1960, **61**, 216-222.

Zajonc, R. B., A note on group judgments and group size. *Human Relations,* 1962, **15**, 177-180.

Zajonc, R. B., Social facilitation. *Science,* 1965, **149**, No. 3681, 269-274.

Zajonc, R. B., *Social psychology: an experimental approach.* Belmont, Calif.: Brooks/Cole, 1966.

Zajonc, R. P., Social facilitation in cockroaches. In E. C. Simmel, R. A. Hoppe, and G. A. Milton (Eds.), *Social facilitation and imitation behavior.* Boston: Allyn and Bacon, 1968.

Zajonc, R. B., and W. Smoke, Redundancy in task assignments and group performance. *Psychometrika,* 1959, **24**, 361-370.

Zajonc, R. B., R. J. Wolosin, M. A. Wolosin, and S. J. Sherman, Individual and group risk-taking in a two-choice situation. *Journal of Experimental Social Psychology,* 1968a, **4**, 89-106.

Zajonc, R. B., R. J. Wolosin, M. A. Wolosin, and J. Sherman, Group risk-taking in a two-choice situation: replication, extension, and a model. Mimeographed paper, Research Center for Group Dynamics, Institute for Social Research, University of Michigan, 1968b.

BCDE79876543210